D1592687

AFRICAN JUNGLE MEMORIES

N.B. AFRICAN BUFFALO TRAILS *is the abridged (and later) version of* HORNED DEATH; *the more complete* HORNED DEATH *contains five more chapters than the later version.*

Author and Friend

AFRICAN JUNGLE
MEMORIES

by

John F. Burger

ILLUSTRATED

SAFARI PRESS, INC.

P.O. BOX 3095, Long Beach, CA 90803

CONTENTS

FOREWORD

African Jungle Memories is compiled from diaries which I kept during my many years of wandering in the African bush. In this volume I have recorded more adventures on the trail of the gorilla, man-eating lions, the buffalo and the elephant, etc.

But every adventure in the forest is not necessarily concerned with the killing of animals. I have often found it more interesting and exciting to watch the behaviour of animals in their natural state than I ever did in killing them.

My observations on the lion, made after many hundreds of hours of close and intimate study, is a terrible indictment against what is generally believed to be such a noble beast. "Nature red in tooth and claw" is an old maxim of the jungle to which no other animal responds more completely than does the lion. But the law of the jungle is not always one of ferocity and destruction. In sharp relief is that other law: the law of love, devotion and solicitude for their young which is highly developed in almost every jungle species, and this also I found an equally interesting study.

A chapter is devoted to the strange women I have met who turned to the forest in order to find the thrills and excitement they failed to find in the conventional life of the city.

Readers are invited to join me at the camp-fires at night, where we discuss not only the events of that day, but also those of the many other days of the past.

JOHN F. BURGER

Palma de Mallorca

CHAPTER I

GORILLA TRAILS

WHEN THE UNINITIATED are discussing hunting adventures they repeatedly argue as to which is the most dangerous animal to hunt. This is a question that cannot be answered satisfactorily even by the hunting fraternity. All the killers in the bush are dangerous creatures, and the outcome of every encounter with any of them will depend on the prevailing conditions at the time and on the skill and anticipation of the hunter.

A question of far greater interest to both the professional and the amateur is: Which is the most *difficult* animal to hunt in the African bush? As in the case of dangerous animals, the list here is also reduced to three or four species. From my own experience, I nominate them in the following order: the gorilla, the okapi and the bongo. All three species are to be found in the Belgian Congo; in the case of the okapi, in the Belgian Congo only. The gorilla's habitat extends far into French Equatorial Africa and they are also to be found in Uganda.

I was very young when I made my first attempt on the gorilla trail, and on that occasion I chose the Birunga range of volcanic mountains in the Kivu. In those days the restrictions were not as severe as they are today, and the official attitude towards gorilla-hunting was more or less: if a man is fool enough to brave the elements, and can survive the most frightful conditions until he can catch up with a family of gorillas, he will have surmounted so many obstacles that it is not necessary to add to his troubles.

In those days the Kivu was one of the most inaccessible parts of Africa. It is possible today to motor in comfort to Lake Kivu—quite close to the volcanic range, but in those days the journey was accomplished on foot through dense forest, in which one's safety was threatened not only by wild animals and the conditions in the forest, but also by savage tribes.

On the occasion of my first attempt I tried my luck along the slopes of the Birungu range, which included Mounts Mikeno, Visoke and Sabeno. We were camped at the foot of the range, from where the imposing spectacle of the three giants was clearly visible. At night the sky along the ridge of the mountains appeared in flaming red colours, and the incessant rumbling of thunder high up on the peaks was clearly audible. During the ten days I spent in that region there was always a thunderstorm raging on the peaks of one or other of the three mountains.

It is in the middle heights of the range that the great anthropoids make their home, in what is probably the densest forest in all Africa. Here, for the most part, we had to hack our way through the dense forest, and the going over the ancient lava-beds was extremely difficult and dangerous.

After I had spent ten days in this wilderness I was lucky to see one big male, and caught only a fleeting glimpse of the other members of the family as they disappeared in the dense forest. In those forests the light was never more than a glimmering twilight. Photography is completely out of the question, and although the occasion did not arise, I felt certain that it would be impossible to train the sights of a rifle on any animal at a distance beyond ten yards—an uncomfortably close distance where a big male gorilla is concerned. That was my first experience in hunting the gorilla, and when I left the Kivu Mountains I was convinced that it would be physically impossible to capture or even photograph the great anthropoids in that region.

It was a good many years later that I met Thomas Barnes, who at that time was probably the chief authority on gorilla-hunting in Africa. I was in close contact with him in the Katanga for many months, and during the numerous discussions we had on the subject I learned from him why my first adventure had ended so unsuccessfully. From what he told me it became obvious that, without a very elaborate and complete organisation at the beginning, no hunter could ever expect to have the same success as he would in hunting other animals. I learned from him also that there were other gorilla haunts in the Congo where conditions were not so utterly impossible as they were in the volcanic range in the Kivu.

One such district was close to what was then the outline of the borders of the National Parc Albert, quite near to the Ituri Forest. There it was possible to organise gangs of experienced native hunters, whose method of hunting the gorilla was to encircle him with their home-made nets. To get such a ponderous organisation to function would take a very long time, and it would be necessary to have a European on the spot to attend to all the details for a successful safari. This would need considerable capital.

I had been in the Congo for some years when a friend, Paul Didier, decided to settle down in the area. I approached him on the subject of organising such an expedition. Paul was keenly interested, and promised to attend to the matter as soon as he had completed his own business as labour recruiter.

It was nearly a year later when he wrote to say he had made sufficient progress to warrant a serious attempt. The area he had chosen for the safari was adjacent to the National Parc. Mostly of dense bamboo forest, it was the type of country favoured by the gorilla. Two months later I set out on my second gorilla trail.

In those days permits were granted only to capture gorillas, and not to kill, except in self-defence. The arrangement suited me admirably, for I had no particular desire to kill any of the big apes, but merely to capture one or two young ones if possible, for at that time as much as five hundred pounds could be obtained for a healthy young specimen.   When I arrived at our point of departure Paul had everything organised for the long trek across country to gorilla land.   There was much enthusiasm among the locally recruited porters, and everyone was looking forward to the great adventure on the trail of the " Zugu-muntu ", as the gorilla is called.

The trek to the point at the edge of the great forest from where the hunt was to start was trying but uneventful, and when we finally landed at our destination nearly three weeks later we decided to rest for a few days.

I was particularly anxious to get all the available information from the local hunters as to the procedure to be adopted.   The next few days were occupied in long discussions about the habits of the gorilla and the methods most likely to succeed in capturing a young one.

Right at the beginning it was made clear to me that although there were several families in the forest, the locating of them would depend entirely on luck.   There was little if any hope of walking on to a family unexpectedly in the dense forest, for visibility there was extremely limited and the gorilla never comes out into the open.   The procedure would be to locate fresh tracks of a family on the move and stick to these—perhaps for days—until we caught up with them.   After that it would be a question of trailing them all day long until nightfall, when they would settle down in a suitable spot for encircling by nets.

There was no question of driving them in any desired direction, for the gorilla is one animal who takes violent exception to being driven.   For a short while they will tolerate such interference, but soon the head of the family, usually a big male standing anything over six feet high and weighing up to 500 lb., will show resentment and turn on his pursuers unexpectedly.   When a big male attacks, it is generally with fatal results to somebody.   The safest thing, they stated, was to pick out the leader as soon as possible after contact was made and get him out of the way with a well-placed bullet.

A suitable spot was any place in the forest where there were not too many large trees to cut down around the area where the nets were to be erected, for these would help the gorillas to clear the nets. The native hunters were possessed of a few muzzle-loaders, and every one of them carried the usual spears, bows and arrows and tins to beat. These pots and tins are beaten at all points around the nets, and as the gorillas give way and group together in the dense forest the nets are drawn in closer, until finally they are drawn so close that the entire family will make a concerted rush and break down the nets in order to escape. That is the moment of greatest danger, but also the most likely opportunity to capture any young ones that may get entangled in the nets during the confusion. The most important thing to do was to watch the big male and keep well out of his way at the moment of the break-through. An obvious weakness in this scheme was the fact that it would be virtually impossible to keep the big fellow under observation, in view of the dense forest and the uncertainty as to where he would choose to make his bid for freedom. Another disconcerting feature was the fact that if trouble started, it would be at such short range as to leave very little time to take suitable precautions.

I listened to all these discussions with the greatest interest, and when the morning came for us to set out on the trail I felt I had a reasonably good knowledge of the procedure to be followed and quite a good inkling of what to expect. Our safari consisted of over two hundred natives. These included porters for our foodstuffs and equipment and the enormous bundles of nets. Large quantities of food also had to be carried for the natives, for in the deep forest where the gorillas lived there was no other game to be found, and even if there was, any indiscriminate shooting there would seriously minimise our chances of catching up with a family. The many porters also would serve a useful purpose in clearing the forest to lay nets and to provide extra noise when the time came to encircle the gorillas.

Our starting point was about ten miles from the forest. The departure was marked by great hilarity, singing and handshakings. That night we camped deep in the forest. During the latter part of the day the scouts had been looking for fresh tracks, of which they found no sign. From there onwards it was a nightmare experience traversing the dense tree and bamboo forests. Every day brought the same results—no fresh trails and no sign of gorillas. Towards the end of the second week we picked up the first comparatively fresh-looking trail, which we followed for two days, but subsequently abandoned, as it led into even more impenetrable forest.

It was early one morning at the beginning of the third week that we came across other fresh tracks, and these we followed. Late in the afternoon two scouts came in to report that they had spotted a family. From now onwards it was our business to stick as close as possible to the trail and wait for the gorillas to settle down at night. Gorillas are not fast travellers and do not cover great distances when on the move. The chief difficulty is to keep in touch with them without alarming them, for they are adepts in the art of taking cover.

We followed this family all the next day, and on two occasions when they grouped together there were long discussions between the natives as to the advisability of laying down the nets immediately. The majority, however, were in favour of waiting until later in the day; thus when, an hour or so before sunset, the family grouped again, the nets were brought out and the entire gang of hunters and porters set to work to encircle them. Up to that stage I had seen no more than a glimpse of shadowy forms moving in the forest, but the natives were quite certain that by the time the nets were finally securely fastened that night the entire family would be safely enclosed.

Early the next morning the drive would begin from the far end; there would be singing and shouting and as much noise as possible, and as the gorillas moved away from the approaching din, the nets would be brought in closer. All round the nets, hunters armed with spears, bows and arrows, and the four muzzle-loaders would take up their positions. Sooner or later during the drive the gorillas were bound to try to break through the nets, but just at which point no one could foretell. That would be the moment of greatest danger, for it is usually the big male who emerges first and clears the way for the rest of the family.

When I went to sleep that night I had serious misgivings about the success of the scheme, in spite of the assurances of the hunters that all would turn out well. Their enthusiasm was no doubt stimulated by the large cash reward that awaited them should they succeed in capturing a young one. To me it all seemed very crude and primitive, and I certainly had no heart for the killing side of the business.

Shortly before daybreak the camp was astir, and with the first streaks of dawn the natives started moving into position. A few more trees had to be cut down, after which all would be ready for the drive. This was the first occasion in my hunting experience when the natives were not very concerned about protection or guidance from the European. Paul and I were told we could take up our positions wherever we liked; no one knew just where the break-through would be made, and it behoved each of us to look out for ourselves and keep out of danger. There was only one point they stressed, and that was to make sure that the big male was accounted for as soon as he was spotted. My friend and I were both armed with heavy-calibre sporting rifles and repeating shotguns loaded with buckshot. For our purpose we figured that the shotguns would be the most reliable. We decided that if the big male should come our way we would shoot to kill only as a last resource.

B

Despite what the natives had told us previously, I was content to rely on the opinion of Barnes, who years before had told me that the noise of rapid fire will keep the big male at bay, but care had to be taken that he was not hurt during the process of firing shots over his head, for that would provoke him into an attack.

A few minutes after we had taken up our positions, pandemonium broke out in the forest towards our right. The natives were singing and shouting and beating their pots with wild abandon. The noise persisted for fully a quarter of an hour before we noticed the first movement in the dense forest in front of us. At that moment two shots rang out quite close to us. On the far side of the net the din was increased, and there also two shots were fired. Suddenly there was a determined rush for the net some ten yards to our left, as the group, now well scattered, crashed into it—the big male in the lead. As the net gave way the natives from the far end closed in; they were behind the fleeing apes. For a few moments all was wild confusion, then once again the big male came into view on our left.

He was coming in our direction at a fairly fast pace and on all fours. Suddenly he stopped, stood erect and started beating his enormous chest. With his jaws wide open he emitted a series of weird, blood-curdling screams and grunts. It was obvious that he had worked himself into a frenzy of rage, and an attack seemed absolutely imminent. We both had him well lined up in our sights and were ready for any emergency, but before he could make his next move I fired two shots over his head. For a moment he seemed undecided and stood looking at us in a menacing attitude, then he turned round and disappeared in the dense undergrowth.

On the far side of the net the natives were still shouting excitedly and chattering among themselves. A few moments later they appeared on the scene with their prize—a baby gorilla. During the confusion he had got entangled in the net along with his mother, but she had quickly freed herself and in her alarm had left him to his fate. I have not sufficient knowledge of gorillas to estimate the age of the baby, but I believe he could not have been much more than three or four months old. The hunt had been a long, costly but exciting adventure, and one baby gorilla was perhaps as much as we could have hoped for. But whatever elation we felt on this subject was short-lived. The baby was determined to have no dealings with any human being. He resented all attempts at friendship on our part and refused to take any food or drink. This may have been due to the fact that he had received internal injuries of which we knew nothing, but he lived for only a few days. This meant that, apart from the adventure and excitement it provided, we had nothing to show for this costly expedition.

It is in view of my experiences on this trip that I consider the gorilla the most difficult animal to hunt. It is quite possible that a better and more scientifically organised expedition will be more successful and have much less trouble. But no one could ever hope to hunt the gorilla successfully without an enormous outlay in cash, and in these days, with the severest restrictions to protect the great apes, there may be even more difficulties to contend with. The most satisfactory feature of our hunt was that no other gorilla was killed. If the big male had come anywhere near the natives who were armed with muzzle-loaders there might have been a different story. As it turned out, he was seen by only the few porters close to us, and although they were armed with spears, they made no attempt to attack him, believing as they did that he would fall to our more modern weapons. The four shots that were fired by the natives were apparently intended to increase the noise in order to drive the gorillas to the far end of the net, for none of the marksmen claimed to have fired at any particular objective, and a careful survey of the area subsequently showed no traces of blood.

So much for the *difficulties* in hunting the gorilla. How does he compare with the buffalo, elephant or lion as a *dangerous* animal? Obviously, one hunt, almost entirely under the guidance of native hunters, is not a sufficiently reliable test to formulate an opinion. From what I saw on this occasion I consider that the gorilla is nothing like so aggressive as any of the above-named animals. The experience related here, if applied to any of them, would without doubt have terminated in a determined charge, for none of them could be kept at bay by harmless gunfire over their heads. It is only a bullet in the right place that could do that. But whatever the gorilla lacks in the matter of aggressiveness is amply compensated for by the conditions in which he has to be hunted, for trouble there has to be settled at the extremely short range of from five to ten yards, and visibility is always bad. It is quite certain that if a big male gorilla should catch up with his tormentor he will kill as effectively as any of the other recognised killers.

What is equally certain is that no buffalo, elephant, or lion could ever stage such a spine-chilling exhibition of fury as the gorilla—on the other hand, none of them will waste any time on such an exhibition. The most dangerous animal in the bush is the one that is capable of killing you and is most likely to catch you off-guard when he has a grievance to settle. It is, of course, quite natural for the natives in these parts to claim that the gorilla is the most dangerous animal on earth; but that is no criterion. The majority of natives in Central and East Africa are convinced that the chameleon is one of the most deadly creatures in the bush.

Of the two other difficult animals I mentioned earlier —the okapi and the bongo—I have no practical experience to fall back on. During the two months I spent in the Ituri forest previously in search of both species I never saw a sign of either. The pygmies and Bambulas of that region were always optimistic, and assured me that it was only a matter of time and patience before we would catch up with an okapi herd, but their hopes were never realised, and as for the bongo, they held out no hopes at all. These animals apparently live in the deepest part of the forest, and by all accounts have a keener sense of hearing and of smell than any other beast in the forest. To my mind, any animal that the Ituri Pygmies fail to hunt down in two months is a very difficult animal to hunt. At all events, neither of these animals can provide the thrills and excitement that may be found on the trail of the gorilla.

CHAPTER II

BUFFALO VENGEANCE

THE NATIVE WHO stood outside my tent door and told of a herd of buffalo that had entered the gorge at the Old Cherida Village in Tanganyika was actually a mouthpiece for the Sultan of the district. The old man had previously invited me to attend an organised hunt, more in the role of spectator than as a participant. The resulting hunt, although not on nearly so large a scale or so barbarous as one I had previously witnessed in the Sira River district, was one of those field days when animals are trapped and surrounded by a ring of fire. That generally happens during the dry season, when the long grass in the valleys and swamps is ready for burning.

In response to the Sultan's earlier invitation, I had arrived on the scene in time to spoil the day's sport. I had immediately got my hunting gang to set fire to the long grass which covered the only exit between the steep mountain and the even steeper banks of the river flowing into the valley below. By the time the Sultan and his hunters were ready to light the fires at strategic points in order to cut off the retreat of the animals, the only exit was wide open as the result of the fires I had started, and most of the animals in the basin managed to escape.

This wilful act of sabotage had made me very unpopular with the old Sultan and the hunting fraternity of his district, and for some weeks they had completely boycotted me. The only help I could get from them was when I had a surplus of meat to carry into camp, and it was more in the hope of sharing in the spoils than with an idea of being helpful that they responded to my appeals on these occasions.

For the Sultan and one of his henchmen to extend a

fresh invitation to share in yet another hunt was some-what puzzling, and the messenger was promptly sub-jected to a thorough examination. Yes, it was quite true, a herd of about thirty buffalo had been driven into the gorge early that morning, and the hunters, armed with muzzle-loaders, had cut off their retreat. The mountain cliffs on both sides were too steep for the animals to negotiate, and sooner or later they would be forced to come out into the open by way of the mouth of the gorge. There was no question of another fire; the only reason they appealed to me for help was that the gorge was very narrow, the grass all round was from ten to twelve feet high, and therefore too dangerous for their marksmen to cover. A herd stampeding for safety might easily kill several of the hunters, even though they might succeed in bagging a few animals. To climb to vantage points on the sides of the mountains would put them beyond effective range; anything over fifty yards, where buffalo are concerned, would be too great a distance for their muzzle-loaders. For me, with my big rifles that could " kill at many thousands of yards ", it would be an easy matter. I could take up a position on a cliff, well out of the danger zone yet within range, and the hunters would vacate the exit, circle round the herd higher up in the gorge, and drive them down to the valley through the mouth of the gorge, which I would cover effectively. It would be easy for me to pick off as many as I wanted from my observation post.

The idea of placing myself in a safe position and taking advantage of animals who had no other means of escape but to run through a hail of lead, savoured more of murder than of hunting, and I promptly turned down the invitation, explaining the reason why. A little while later my head tracker, Ndege, was back at the tent door.

" Bwana, if you are thinking of being kind to those buffalo by refusing to shoot them, you are making a big mistake. These people are determined to get their share of the meat, and that messenger fellow has just been

telling us that they are going to burn the herd out. Last
year they did the same thing, and got four calves, but the
District Commissioner got to hear about it and six men
were sent to gaol for long terms.   It is because they are
afraid of more trouble with the police that they have sent
to you for help.   If you do not go they will certainly set
the grass alight.   Perhaps it will be better if you went
there and shot just one or two buffalo and give them a
good share of the meat."

Ndege was right.   If I did not accept the invitation
and help them to satisfy their craving for meat, they
would do the next best thing—despite the consequences.
I sent for the messenger again and after some discussion
I called for my trackers and gun-bearers and we were
on our way to the Cherida Gorge, six miles from my
camp, where we arrived shortly after 3 p.m.   The setting
was very much as the messenger had described it, and
the passage was blocked by four hunters with muzzle-
loaders and a dozen or more natives, armed with pots
and pans, which they beat at regular intervals to keep
the herd away from the exit.

There was only one point in the messenger's story at
variance with the true state of affairs, and that was his
statement that the grass surrounding the gorge was ready
for burning.   There was, in fact, no grass at all, but a
dense mass of green river reeds, ten or more feet high,
which extended for fully a mile down to the valley below.
No ordinary fire would ever burn down that tangled
mass of reeds.   The threat of burning the buffaloes out,
therefore, could not be put into operation for at least
another six weeks or two months, when the reeds would
be dry enough to burn.   However, I had come all that
way, and, as in the case of the Sultan and his men, my
natives, as usual, were spoiling for a meat feast.

A more careful survey of the position helped to ease
my conscience, for the position from which I would
cover the exit was fully 200 yards away, and the clearance
through which the herd would have to pass did not

measure much more than thirty yards. If the herd
came through that clearing in mass formation and at
top speed, I would be very lucky to place more than two
or three shots of doubtful value, as there were several
obstructions in the line of fire.

It was shortly before 5 p.m. when I finally took up my
position and the drive from the top end of the gorge
began. Sitting there, perched on a cliff, I could hear
the herd grunting and bellowing as they made for the
narrow exit; a few minutes later the first members broke
cover. A particularly fine bull offered a good target,
and I could hear the bullet strike after I squeezed the
trigger. It was not part of my business to watch the
effect of my shot—the trackers and spotters would take
care of that. Following close on the heels of the big
bull were several cows and calves, and these I allowed to
pass. Then another magnificent bull broke cover; a
second later he collapsed with a bullet through the neck.
A few more cows and calves made up the rest of the
herd, and these I allowed to go their way. The excitement was all over.

" We have two fine big bulls, and that should give
you folks all the meat you need for a while," I remarked
to Ndege as I handed him my rifle.

" That last bull seems to be dead, Bwana," he replied,
" but the first one got up again; he is badly wounded
and he has entered the long reeds down there. I do not
think he will go very far because he fell like a sack of
meal when you hit him, and he was limping badly when
I saw him last as he entered the grass."

" Are you sure he was limping, Ndege? " I queried.

" Oh, yes, Bwana, he was limping badly in his front
left leg; I think his shoulder is broken."

A limp in the front leg, a fractured shoulder, and he
had entered that tangle of long reeds and dense undergrowth! It was one of those touchy situations in buffalo-
hunting that one prefers to read about rather than have
to cope with! The very best I could hope for was that

the bull had shipped a bullet through one, or both, lungs. If he was limping in the front leg it was very unlikely, in view of the angle of my shot, that the heart was attained, and equally doubtful whether the second lung had been hit. For the moment, however, first things came first, and that was to make quite sure that the second bull was dead and attended to; after that I would examine the blood trail of the wounded animal and see what that would show us.

The second bull was dead without a doubt; he had gone down to a ·404 slug through the neck which had fractured the vertebrae. In addition to his bulk, he carried a pair of magnificent horns with a forty-two inches spread and correspondingly fine bosses. I was anxious to preserve the trophy for a mask, and it was quite half an hour later before that part of the business was attended to. It was now nearly six o'clock, and I called on Ndege and Abele, my two trackers, to help me follow the trail of the wounded animal.

At the spot where he had taken cover there were only a few spots of blood on the undergrowth; a few yards farther on the trail we found the first large splotch of heavy blood. I examined it carefully; there was no doubt, the bull was bleeding from the lungs; but a careful examination of his tracks at this point indicated that he was still travelling at a fairly good speed—a fast trot, if not a gallop. A wounded bull in country where visibility extends for only about ten feet, and the dense reeds were more than ten feet high, contains all the explosive qualities of a load of dynamite, and any attempt to follow the trail into that death-trap would have been the height of folly. In less than an hour the sun would go down, and I still had to arrange for a suitable spot for my camp for the night. Both Ndege and the other tracker, Abele, agreed with me that it would be best to leave the bull until the next day and then decide what would be best to do.

As we walked back on the trail we met the four village

hunters with their muzzle-loaders. They were busy examining the first heavy deposit of blood, and were wildly excited.

" He's dead, Bwana; by now he is stiff. When they throw up blood like that they don't go very far. We'll have him in a few minutes," the leader continued, as they were getting ready to follow the blood trail.

I immediately called them back and got Ndege to explain to them just what to expect if the bull was still alive and capable of putting up a fight. At weaving webs of truth and untruth where buffalo are concerned Ndege is absolutely peerless. Not only did he have more than twenty years of experience to draw upon, he had also an extremely fertile imagination. As he took them through some of the gruesome experiences he himself had survived in similar circumstances, they stood listening to him wide-eyed and awe-stricken.

" If you are tired of life, my friends, that is the right road to follow," he finished as he pointed towards the blood trail.

With that we all returned to the carcass and, after seeing that the head and horns were properly attended to, I left instructions for the meat to be carried to a spot where I intended to camp for the night. After that my two trackers and I proceeded to the spot to prepare camp. A few minutes later the head and the first loads of meat were brought in and the porters returned for the remainder.

It was whilst we were busy tying the head to a heavy branch that we were startled by loud screaming and shouting which came from the direction of the carcass; this was followed by the fleeing gang, running towards us at top speed.

" Kafuli is dead, Bwana," shouted the first one to reach us.

Soon the rest of the gang was crowding in on us.

" Yes, yes," shouted another, " Kafuli is certainly dead, for he did not shout again for help."

It took a minute or two to calm the panic-stricken natives and obtain a coherent account of the trouble. It appeared that Ndege's warning did not sink in deep enough, and almost immediately after we had left the carcass, Kafuli, one of the hunters, had gone back to follow the blood trail. For a while all was silent, then there was a loud bellowing and grunting, followed by screams which ceased suddenly. At that moment they took off for safety and the bellowing and grunting could still be heard. They felt quite certain that the bull had got Kafuli, and the fact that he had suddenly stopped shouting indicated that the bull had killed him. On the other hand, the fact that the bull kept on grunting and bellowing might mean that Kafuli had climbed a tree and that the bull was menacing him from below.

I had no illusions about that subject at all, and felt certain that Kafuli never had time to find safety in the tree-tops. So there it was—the daylight was already beginning to fade, in the dense reed-bed barely a mile from us lay a dead native with an infuriated buffalo bull in close attendance. Kafuli had stubbornly refused to listen to wiser counsels, and had brought all this trouble on himself. I certainly had no intention of walking into that hornet's nest to investigate. In any case, I had not the slightest doubt that the native was dead. The fact that the bull had kept on grunting and bellowing after Kafuli had stopped shouting for help had an ominous and familiar sound about it. In his frenzy, the bull was then giving the corpse a final savage mauling, and the bellowing was merely a vocal expression of his rage.

For the remainder of that night there was little rest, for the natives sat in a group around the camp-fire, loudly bewailing the evil fortune that had befallen their brother. The only consoling words I heard that night came from the head of the community:

" Tomorrow we will find him. Perhaps he is not

dead, and the bwana will help us to kill that vicious brute."

I did not trouble to discuss the matter, or to ask them just how they expected me to " kill the vicious brute ". For me it was sufficient to know that there was a killer buffalo in an impregnable position, ready to exact further vengeance whilst he was able to do so, and I certainly had no intention of endangering my own life as well as that of others in an attempt to flush the bull out of hiding.

Early the next morning the gang were back at the spot where the second bull had fallen in the open clearing the previous day. Here they had all mounted trees and sat shouting for Kafuli. Following the example of the natives, I had also mounted one of the higher trees. If the bull showed up, well and good. If not, I would leave him where he was—dead or alive—and await further developments.

" What are we going to do now, Bwana? " queried one of the natives next to me.

" We are going to send you, or any other willing fool, in there and see just how long it will take the bull to kill you. If no one is willing to go and investigate, we will sit here and wait for the vultures to tell us what is happening," I replied.

It was shortly after 11 a.m. before the first vulture descended upon a nearby tree and sat staring at a fixed spot on the ground ahead of him. Soon there were several scores more, but they all remained in the tree staring in the same direction. Occasionally they became restive and fluttered their wings, but none descended to the ground; until such time as they did, we all knew that there was still danger threatening. We also knew that whenever these loathsome birds congregated at a spot, as they were doing now, death is never long delayed. It was well after 3 p.m. before the first vulture descended and settled in the long reeds; a few minutes later the others followed suit. I fired two shots at the spot where they were congregating, but there was only a fluttering of wings in response. Shortly after that we could hear the sounds of raucous voices as they fought for the spoils.

I had handed Ndege and Abele a rifle each, whilst I carried a heavy ·425; accompanied by the three village hunters, whose muzzle-loaders were fully charged, we walked slowly in the direction of the squawking birds. Nearer and nearer we came to the spot; then, suddenly, there was a loud fluttering of wings as the vultures took off. It was a tense moment, but there was no cause for alarm, for at the spot they had so hurriedly vacated lay the carcass of the bull. A few yards farther away was the mutilated corpse of Kafuli. In keeping with his vindictive nature, the bull had savagely gored him and left several gaping wounds in his body. After that he had crushed the skull to a pulp with his heavy hooves. Kafuli's corpse was one of the most gruesome examples of buffalo fury I had ever seen.

Subsequent examination of the buffalo carcass confirmed my opinion of the previous day. The bullet had missed the heart by a few inches, ploughed through the one lung, and lodged in the breast-bone. Thus, although mortally wounded, it took him a long time to die, but in those intervening hours he had enough vitality—and devil—left in him to kill a dozen men.

Just what made Ndege think he had seen the bull limping badly and that the shoulder was fractured I will never understand. Native observation, no matter from how experienced a quarter, is always of a doubtful quality. At the time of this incident, Ndege, the finest tracker I ever knew, had been with me for nearly twenty years, and had been in at the kill of many hundreds of buffaloes; but, as on several previous occasions when events got exciting, reliable observation was replaced by a lively imagination. It was as the result of the most " careful and reliable observation " by native spotters that I once walked into an ambush whilst on the trail of a wounded buffalo and escaped death by the proverbial skin of my teeth. That experience had taught me never to rely too much on the judgement or observation of even the most experienced natives when such dangerous situations arise.

CHAPTER III

LIONS HAVE RIGHT-OF-WAY

To my mind the greatest fascination of the bush is that conditions never remain static for very long. The man who catches the 8 a.m. bus for the office every morning and who can tell beforehand just what will happen during the day, and feel content with such a scheme of things, has always been a puzzle to me.

That modern progress is due to the fact that there are millions of such people all over the world is undoubtedly true, and I have no doubt that they have contributed far more towards the advance of mankind than the man who sallies forth into the bush every morning, rifle in hand, and asks himself the question, " What will this day bring forth? " For myself, the uncertainty of the bush has always had a great appeal to me. The mere prospect of excitement and adventure has generally proved sufficient compensation even on the days when I walked a score or more miles and saw nothing more exciting than a lizard making a dash for safety—it is unfortunately true that every denizen of the African bush will flee from the presence of man, the deadliest killer of them all.

During the latter part of the last war I was responsible for supplies for a concern engaged on high priority war work, and in their various installations they employed some two thousand natives. This property operated in Northern Tanganyika, in one of the worst tsetse-infested areas in Africa. Apart from the occasional chicken to be found in a native village, no other domestic animal survived for long in these parts, and here, as in every other Central African territory I ever knew, the natives were always meat hungry.

To supply two thousand natives with sufficient game-meat to satisfy this meat craze was quite an undertaking. During the dry season I somehow managed to keep the pot boiling reasonably well, for in the Lake Katavi area, and in the vast plains beyond, game was quite plentiful. At Lake Katavi itself it was not an unusual sight to see herds of over five hundred buffaloes coming to drink—one immense herd I saw near the lake one morning exceeded a thousand head. In the circumstances it was not too difficult to keep the camp supplied with buffalo meat, for apart from being an excellent meat provider, the buffalo, owing to the spread of the tsetse-fly, of which he is a carrier, was put on the vermin list, and not subject to game restrictions.

It was in the Lake Katavi area that I had some of my most hair-raising experiences with buffaloes, and that included the occasion when an enormous bull appeared suddenly and charged the three-ton truck on which we were carrying the proceeds of the day's hunt. It was just before sunset, and not expecting to see any more game, I had packed up my rifles for the day. By the time I was able to unpack them and attend to the bull, he had gone a long way towards demolishing the front part of the truck. Both headlamps had been torn away, an eight-inch hole had been driven through the radiator by one of his enormous horns. I was sitting on top of the hood of the truck, and at the moment I fired for his brain he was busy demolishing one of the front mudguards.

Whilst all this was going on, the Italian prisoner-of-war driver, Biondi, and his assistant, Mutali, a Swahili native, sat petrified in the front seat screaming for help at the top of their voices. I have often wondered why, in time of danger, people will so readily call on their mothers for help? For whilst Biondi was appealing loudly to " *Mio Madre* ", Mutali was calling equally loudly for " *Mama Yangu* " to come to the rescue.

This old bull, as it turned out, had plenty of reason

c

to be at war with the world. After the excitement was over I examined the carcass, and found no less than five slugs embedded in his body. Over four of them the skin had grown again and, apart from the fact that they were unpleasant souvenirs that helped to fan the flames of resentment, they could not have caused him very much pain. The fifth, however, deeply embedded in his shoulder, was a large jagged piece of iron, obviously fired from a native muzzle-loader, and this had set up a ghastly festering sore.

Apart from a little upset like this, the day's hunt around Lake Katavi generally ensured a good meat supply. But this was during the dry season, when the grass was burnt down and hunting comparatively easy. Once the rainy season had set in there was no more question of hunting, for the grass all round Lake Katavi then grew to twelve or more feet high. Water being plentiful in other areas, the large herds seldom frequented the lake. It was necessary then to go farther afield for meat supplies.

The Ufipa country, some 150 miles from our property, was a profitable field; the vast, undulating plains on the plateau, 4,000 feet above sea level, were free from tsetse, and good cattle-country. Here, on occasions, I was able to buy as many as one hundred and fifty head of cattle, which would be driven to the property and killed on arrival and the meat properly smoked and dried. This was a precaution against the tsetse, for once an animal is infected by tsetse-fly it loses weight at an alarming rate, and the meat soon becomes unfit for human consumption.

The Ufipa country, for the greater part, was barren so far as game was concerned, but for all that, I had some strange and exciting adventures there whilst out on cattle-buying missions. At one stage the road between our property and Ufipa is hacked out through mountainous country for a distance of more than two miles. The grade in some of the straight stretches is as steep as one foot in every twelve, and on both sides of the road the banks are from twenty to thirty feet high.

It was as we were coming down one of these steep inclines one dark night on a five-ton truck fully loaded with vegetables and maize, and with a dozen natives on board, that we ran into a spot of bother. Biondi the Italian was again in the driving-seat, and I was sitting beside him. In view of the steep gradient, we were travelling at about fifteen miles per hour; as we took a bend in the road we suddenly became aware of two dark figures running in the road in front of us. For a moment I thought they were hyenas, but as the full glare of the headlights fell upon them we could see that it was a lion and lioness.

Biondi immediately slammed the brakes on with full force. For a moment the truck dragged on all four wheels and all but came to a stop; then, suddenly, it started rolling down the escarpment, gaining speed rapidly. The sudden violent application of the brakes had burst a cup in the main cylinder of the brake system, and all we had to depend on now was the hand-brake. But the load was too heavy and the incline too steep for the hand-brake to control, and we were rapidly gaining on the two lions as they galloped down the road ahead of us between the two steep banks. My rifles were packed away in the back of the truck, and even with a rifle in hand I would not have been able to do much from a fast-moving truck in the dark. By now the lions were running at high speed, with the truck hot on their heels. At the back of us pandemonium had broken out amongst the natives, for they were sitting out in the open shouting for us to bring the truck to a stop—not realising that we were unable to do so. Beside me Biondi was again appealing to *Mio Madre* to come to the rescue and letting out a torrent of words of which I understood nothing. When the trouble started we quickly took the precaution of closing both windows, but now there was a crashing of glass as Black, my old gun-bearer, smashed the window in order to hand me a rifle. The rifle was about as much use to me as a tennis ball, for a chance shot in the circumstances may have wounded one of the lions and thus aggravated the trouble; besides, it would have been quite impossible for me to sight a gun in the dark.

That mad race on the heels of two lions lasted for fully a mile before the banks tapered down sufficiently for the lions to get clear. When eventually we managed to bring the truck to a stop, both animals had disappeared in the dark and I was quite happy to leave them to go their way. Black, believing that it was a joke I had played in keeping the truck hot on the heels of the two lions, was loud in his denunciation of me and refused to believe that it was a mechanical defect that had prevented us from bringing the truck to a stop. For the rest of that night he refused to speak to me, and accused me of having deliberately risked their lives for my amusement.

We had not seen the last of what I believe were the same two lions, for the following night we had one hundred and fifty head of cattle herded in an enclosure; late that night the enclosure was raided by lions, the herd broke out, and immediately stampeded in the direction of Lake Katavi. It all happened so suddenly that I was unable to get in a shot, for in the dark there were scores of cattle eyes reflected in the beams of my shooting lamp and it was impossible to distinguish these from the eyes of any lion.

Early the next morning we set out on the trail of the herd, and by 3 p.m. my worst fears were confirmed, when we came across the remains of an ox, and the indications were all there to show that the cattle had joined up with a herd of buffalo and made for forest country thirty miles away. For the next eight days we walked all of 200 miles to try to separate the cattle from the buffalo. Every time the buffalo sighted or scented us, they made off at high speed with the dumb oxen following on their trail.

To isolate the two herds presented me with one of the most difficult and tiring jobs I ever had to face in the bush; the only compensation was that I was able to bag two or three buffalo each day whilst we were on the trail. But that, in turn, presented us with more trouble and work, for to follow the trail of a mixed herd of cattle and buffalo during the day, dissecting the enormous carcasses at night, and preparing the meat for the smoking ramps, was a job of considerable magnitude. By the time I finally landed back in camp with the herd of cattle I had been on the road a fortnight longer than I had expected. When, two days later, the remaining fifty head which had not yet been slaughtered again escaped and their tracks led straight for Lake Katavi, it became painfully obvious to me that I was in for another job of cattle-herding. I decided to take my annual short leave and try my luck with elephant. The next fortnight provided me with two glaring examples of just how bad hunters' luck can be at times.

On this trip I was accompanied by Freddie, a young employee recently out from England. He had never hunted before and begged me to take him along. That first week we did our daily quota of twenty-five to thirty miles on the elephant trail. It was late on the afternoon of the eighth day before we came up with the first worthwhile bull in close forest.

When I sat down to line that bull up in my sights at a distance of only about thirty yards, I felt absolutely certain that we would collect him within a few seconds. But it was one of my off-days, the shot was badly placed in the head, and the bull made off at a terrific speed. There was no blood trail to follow and we spent the rest of the afternoon and all the next day looking for the wounded animal without success. The elephant trail was proving too tiresome and disappointing, and I decided to try for buffalo.

We were soon settled down in good buffalo country, and did well for the rest of the time. On our last morning my friend thought he would like to take a few natives and wander off on his own. Having warned him to be careful I left him to go his way and I set off on my own.

About an hour after we had left camp I heard two shots in the distance. I waited for a while, and since there was no shouting and screaming, as there would have been in case of an accident, I went on my way. A few minutes later I dropped a young bull and decided to return to camp.

When I arrived there the natives informed me that my friend had sent for porters to bring in a buffalo he had shot. An hour later the first porters arrived with an enormous head suspended over a pole. I was immediately attracted by the large spread of horns, and quickly got out my steel tape to measure the size—to find a spread of forty-nine inches, which at that time was very close to a world's record. In all my forty years in the bush, during which time I had accounted for more than a thousand buffaloes, the largest pair of horns I ever collected measured only forty-four inches. Freddie, in his first outing, had collected a magnificent trophy, and I helped him to prepare the mask. His luck held good, for a few months later a wealthy American engineer who had come to visit the property, paid him three hundred pounds for the horns.

In the hunting business one is never envious of another's good luck, but I could not help thinking that I was dealt a bad card that morning, for it was on my suggestion that my friend took the direction he did. That was one bit of bad luck for me, but even worse was to follow, for a few days after we got back to camp I heard that the natives of a nearby village had found the carcass of the elephant I had wounded that afternoon.

The tusks measured over seven feet and weighed 131 and 134 lb., respectively; they were immediately claimed by the Game Department as a government trophy!

With two such rough deals in a fortnight, I sat down and thought things over carefully and decided to go back to the cattle-herding business.

Much later in the year I received a letter from the American engineer who had bought Freddie's trophy. In it he told of how he had the head mounted and how the eyes could be lit up at night by electric bulbs. He had given the pupils a reddish tint to give the same effect as they have when the bull is in full charge—" just as you described it to me ". His letter closed by asking me to try my best to find him another pair of about equal size to match the one on his wall. I did not think it worthwhile to tell him that I had walked the bush for nearly forty years in order to see someone else land such a trophy and that it may be another forty years before someone else will show me again just how it is done.

CHAPTER IV

ELEPHANT FURY

"THAT BIG BULL is not only a killer and a raider, he has a devil inside him who helps him to keep clear of trouble. Here we have been walking in circles on his trail for more than a week without even seeing him, and yesterday afternoon he killed two men at Shauri-tenga's village. A runner has just come in to report, and the headman wants you to come over and see if we can run him down this time."

Ndega, my old tracker, was the speaker, and the news was alarming indeed. Quite ten days earlier we had landed in this area to listen to a story of cunning aggression seldom attained by any raider elephant. The bull had been terrorising the district for many weeks. In turn he would raid three of the surrounding villages dotted over the district at distances of ten to twelve miles apart. Not only had he killed three men before we arrived on the scene, he had, in addition, laid most of the plantations bare, and, not satisfied with that, he had taken to breaking down the grass huts in which the natives stored their maize reserves. With the plantations almost completely destroyed and reserves seriously reduced, the outlook was grim indeed. And now there was this final outrage of two men killed.

From the runner's account it appeared that the bull was seen in the plantation late in the afternoon. A number of hunters had loaded their old muzzle-loaders and taken up a position at the bottom end of the plantation, whilst most of the villagers had gone to the top end with pots, pans, and tins which they would beat with wild abandon and drive the raider on to the waiting guns. The elephant had upset all their plans by turning on the beaters, and in quick time two men were tossed and trampled to death.

Usually, when elephants became troublesome and raided plantations, the village headman would send a report to the nearest District Commissioner, who would then take the necessary steps to rid the villagers of their unwelcome visitor. In the present case the matter had been duly reported, and a game scout had come out and destroyed what was believed to be the raider. It transpired later, however, that the scout had killed a " traveller " elephant, whilst the real culprit remained at large. Subsequent appeals had been ignored as the Commissioner believed it was a well-thought-out plan to secure a good supply of elephant meat.

From a hunter's point of view, shooting raider elephants in the Congo was anything but a profitable business. In the first place, official sanction had to be obtained, and this was not always easy. Shooting a raider on an elephant licence was perfectly in order, but a licence at the time cost all of thirty pounds, and in most cases the yield of ivory was not worth the time and powder expended. I had allowed myself to be talked into trailing this bull on the solemn assurance that he carried an enormous pair of tusks, and as I still had one elephant on my licence, I decided to take a sporting chance. All the evidence of the bull's handiwork was there for me to see. The inhabitants would in a short time face starvation if the brute was not curbed, and in addition there was every likelihood of more fatal accidents if the natives should attempt to protect their crops from the raider.

For fully a week we had been walking in circles, as Ndega termed it, following reports of the bull's activity from one village to another. It was in the midst of the dry season, the country was hilly, and the ground so hard that trailing was extremely difficult. Ndega and Abele, my two trackers, were men who could hold their own against any other tracker in the country, but their best efforts had availed us nothing, and the nearest we had come to making contact with the bull was late one afternoon when we came across some fresh droppings. The trail led into hilly country, and by sunset there was still no sign of the bull. The half-hour or so of daylight remaining was barely sufficient to see us back on the main footpath leading to camp. Once again the trail had to be abandoned. That day we had walked all of thirty miles, and it was near midnight before we finally reached camp.

The heavy going on the three previous days had so utterly fatigued me that I decided to spend the next day in camp to rest. It was shortly after 9 a.m. when a runner arrived to inform me that the bull had that night raided the very village we had left the previous morning, and that at the time of his departure the brute was standing sleeping under a big tree not far from the scene of his depredations of the previous night. The hunters in the village had thought it best to leave the bull alone and wait for me to come and deal with him.

An hour later we were once more on the trail of the troublesome beast, but when we arrived at the spot three hours later there was once again no sign of the bull. Again the entire afternoon was spent in fruitless trailing, and as on the previous day, it was almost midnight when we got back to camp.

The next day passed without incident and we were all glad of the opportunity of a welcome rest. The following morning the natives were still tired and sulky, and I decided, in the absence of more reports of trouble, to spend another day in camp, and replenish our meat supplies in the afternoon. Game was plentiful in the district, but the fear of shooting and frightening the bull away—should he be in the vicinity—had reduced our meat supplies to a minimum, and this was responsible for the surly attitude of the porters and trackers.

At ten o'clock that morning yet another messenger came in to report the presence of the bull at Kandabele's village, nine miles away. This time the bull had apparently gone berserk, for not only did he trample down a large patch of maize, he had actually entered the village and sent the natives skeltering into their huts to escape his wrath. One native had been tossed; the runner did not know whether he was fatally injured or not. He himself had waited for an opportunity when the bull was at the far end of the village, and had then taken a chance to emerge from his hut to come and call me. He feared that the bull might pull down some of the huts to get at the occupants.

" He must be ill, or suffering from toothache, for him to run about so madly, screaming at the top of his voice," he concluded.

Ironically, the few natives possessed of muzzle-loaders had that morning left for Shauri-tenga's village in search of their enemy.

This was an alarming state of affairs; the rogue bull had now taken to raiding the village as well as the plantation, and if, as the runner suggested, he was suffering from toothache, there was no telling what extremes the beast would go to on his trail of destruction. A few minutes later we were once again on the way to the latest scene of trouble. I had small hopes of finding the bull at the village by the time we arrived there, for we had a good ten miles to walk. It was close on 3 p.m. when we could see the village in the distance.

When we had approached to within 200 yards of the outskirts I signalled for my natives to stop. In the village all was silent. Could it be that the bull was still menacing the villagers? More likely, I thought, they were having a siesta in the heat of the day. I decided, however, to approach the village on the assumption that the bull was still there. I handed my ·425 heavy-calibre rifle to Ndega and instructed him to circle around to the left. I myself kept a ·333 medium rifle, and my gun-bearer carried a double-barrelled ·450 express. He was instructed to stick close on my heels and hand me the rifle should I need it. We approached the village in dead silence, taking advantage of every bit of cover we

could find.   We had now reached the first line of huts.
All was silent.

Looking up towards the far end of the village, I was
suddenly aware of a movement.   Yes, there it was again!
The bull was leaning against a big tree near a native
hut.   But already he had picked up our scent and started
to spread his ears.   Instinctively I put out my hand for
the heavy-calibre rifle.   A second, two seconds, three
seconds, and there was still no response.   On looking
back I saw the gun-bearer sitting some fifty yards behind
me; he was busy extracting a thorn from his foot!   The
bull was already showing signs of aggressiveness, and I
heartily cursed my stupidity in landing myself in this
desperate position.   There was only one thing to do,
and that was to go into action with the lighter rifle before
the bull started his charge.   It was sound judgement,
for as the third bullet struck him in the chest he swerved
round and made for the forest.

With the comparative light rifle I had used there was
no way of telling what damage I had inflicted.   The
chances were overwhelmingly in favour of my having
done nothing more than penetrate deeply into the flesh.
The resulting smarting pain would account for the bull's
sudden flight.   It was at that moment that the gun-
bearer came rushing up with my elephant gun!

For an experienced hunter, I had committed the
greatest folly imaginable, the kind of folly that has
landed many a careless hunter six feet under.   The slip
had cost me dearly, but I considered myself lucky to
have lost nothing more than a prize trophy.   The
indications now were that I had once again reached a
stalemate.   Both trackers were totally averse to trailing
the bull into close forest.   Along the few yards we had
followed the trail in open country there was a heavy
blood trail, but it was obvious that the blood came from
deep flesh wounds.   The heart or lungs had not been
attained.   Once the trail entered dense forest I was
compelled to call a halt, for the natives, with every

justification, all refused to follow that trail. The position now was as bad as could possibly be imagined. The injury to which I had subjected the bull would rankle in his brain and aggravate his ill temper, and there was no telling just how he would react. Still, there was not much I could do to improve the position. I was tired and disappointed, and the only thing to do was to return to camp and await further developments.

It was two days later that a runner came in to report the events I have described at the beginning of my narrative. The fact that I had loaded the bull with lead after he had raided Katambele's village and that he had exacted vengeance at Shauri-tenga's village the day after, inclined me to the belief that he would select Katunga's village for his next outrage. I decided I would go there and stay, for a week, if necessary, and await further developments.

Late that afternoon we were camped on the outskirts of Katunga's kraal, and all the porters and trackers were instructed to keep a sharp look-out for the raider. That night we slept peacefully, for the bull failed to put in an appearance. Early the next morning scouts took up their positions all round the village.

It was shortly after 3 p.m. that one of them came in to report the presence of the bull. Sitting high up in a tree, he had watched the brute take up his position under a big tree a hundred yards or so from him. He had sat waiting until the bull had gone to sleep and then quietly made his way back to camp to report.

" This time you are sure to find him, Bwana, for I am certain he is fast asleep and will not move away until it gets cooler."

This time, I decided, I would take the trail with my heaviest gun in my own hands. Ndege would carry the other heavy calibre and Abele the lighter ·333. The trail was on, and I felt certain that only the most unexpected mishap could possibly bring about another failure. Half an hour later we reached the tree from which the scout had made his observation. As he pointed to a large tree away to the right, I spotted the bull, still standing sleeping. With both Ndega and Abele close on my heels, we crept to within thirty yards of the bull, and came to a stop.

He was still fast asleep and blissfully unaware of the imminent danger that threatened him. But all was not lost for him, he still had a slim sporting chance of survival, for there is an old tradition of the forest which every serious hunter respects, and that is never to kill a sleeping animal. I crept up silently to a bush not more than twenty yards from him, and resting my gun on one of the larger branches, I sat down for a few moments to recover from my snake-like crawl, then I slowly raised my rifle and manoeuvred him into my sights until I had him safely covered.

I whistled loudly and counted: One, two, three. The big bull was still standing sniffing the air when a ·450 express bullet ploughed into his brain and he rolled over—dead. His trail of violence and destruction had come to an end. The temptation must have proved too great for my two gun-bearers, for the huge carcass had hardly hit the ground when two more shots rang out close behind me.

As I had suspected, the tusks were very much overrated, but they yielded 87 and 90 lb. respectively, and although that amount of ivory represented no fortune, it repaid me handsomely for my time and trouble.

Within a few minutes there was a wild scramble for the meat, and every inhabitant of that village was equipped with a knife, a panga or an axe. For a while I feared that serious injuries might result from their eagerness to secure their share of the spoils. In this frantic rush to get at the carcass I firmly believe they were prompted not so much by their anxiety to appease their craving for meat, as a desire to enjoy the privilege of crunching the flesh of their arch-enemy between their teeth. That night there was wild celebration, for the natives from the surrounding villages had heard the news and were already on the spot.

" Tomorrow night the beer will be ready," announced Katunga, the village headman; " the bwana will drink the first cup, we will sing, we will dance, we will pay tribute to brave men."

Yes, they would dance, they would sing and pay tribute. I knew exactly what that meant. The entire beer supplies from all three villages would be pooled, and there would be a hilarious drunk for a week or more, in which my trackers and porters would join. I had already lost too much time in this neighbourhood and could not remain for this lengthy celebration. Early the next morning I called for Ndege.

" Tell your men to get ready and collect their share of the meat, for in an hour's time we must be on our way," I said.

" But, Bwana, you heard what Katunga said last night? We are going to celebrate; there will be beer and dancing. Where do you wish us to go in such a hurry? "

" I do not know, Ndege, I do not know just where we shall go. We will follow the trail and find out what awaits us at the next bend in the road." Little did I know that the " next bend " would provide one of my most thrilling bush adventures.

That night I was lying in my tent; nearby the camp-fire burnt brightly, the flesh-pots were full, and Ndege was in great vein, giving the events of the previous day a thorough going over.

" If I had dared to speak loudly I would have shouted and asked him if he intended to kiss that big brute before shooting him. Did you see the way he crawled like a snake to get closer? Eh, eh, my friends, I assure you his luck will not last for ever and before long he will come to a bad end."

"You do not understand, Ndege," rejoined Abele. "These white people have *mooti* which protects them from danger. Many years ago I hunted with a *Mawrastag* [Afrikaner] and he told me all about it. Why, I saw him follow a man-eating lion on bare feet in the middle of the night and kill it. Nothing ever happened to him, and when he died it was from a bad disease."

"Perhaps you are right, Abele," replied Ndege. "Every now and again I see the bwana put *mooti* on all his guns. He keeps it in a bottle in his haversack. [A compound to prevent guns from rusting.] But it is good for us to remember that we have no *mooti* like that and sooner or later he will lead us into a lot of trouble."

I was dead tired and did not hear the rest of the conversation as I dropped off into a deep sleep and dreamed of a killer elephant. Early the next morning Ndege was at my door.

"A runner has arrived, Bwana. He walked all the way to Katunga's village yesterday in the hope of finding us there. For the best part of the night he has followed our trail. He tells a bad story of a man who was taken by a man-eater only two days ago. Perhaps you will talk to him and listen to what he has to say?"

"Yes, send him in, Ndege; I will listen to his story."

The runner was ushered in, and during the next ten minutes I listened to one of the most gruesome stories of a man-eating lion.

"Get the safari ready to leave as soon as possible," I told Ndege. "We have reached 'the next bend' in the road."

CHAPTER V

THE MAN-EATERS OF SANDOA

THE MESSENGER WHO had come from Katunga's village that morning with an appeal for help from the village headman, Mulenga, had an alarming story to tell. Mulenga had sent him the morning after a man-eating lion had carried off a woman with a child on her back, just before sunset the previous day.

" We have been having trouble with lions in our village ever since I was a little boy," said the runner. " If it is not our men and women they carry off, it is our livestock. I can remember at least ten of our people being carried off by lions during the last few years. We have killed four of the devils so far, the last one more than a year ago. That one we killed with spears after he had entered the hut of one of our men, and was busy carrying the man out by the door when we closed in on him. Yes, Bwana, that was a terrible night, for as soon as the man screamed for help we all rushed to the hut with our spears. Two men were badly injured during the fight, and the one in the hut was killed, but when it was all over the lion had a hundred spears sticking in his skin.

" For nearly a year after that we had peace, but now, during the past few weeks, the trouble has started all over again, but this time it is worse than before, for the lion never enters the village, but lies in wait near the footpaths and attacks without warning. Each time it is in a different direction, and the only way we can get water and firewood to our village is for hunters to accompany the women. There are not enough hunters to accompany all the women in different directions, and now it is time for us to collect our maize crops. The woman who was taken the other day was returning from her plantation, where she had worked all day. As soon as we got the news a big party of men went out after the lion, but at sunset they had to give up the chase. Early the next morning we found the remains of the woman and her child. We knew that you were at Katunga's village, and Mulenga told me to go there and ask you to come and help us. I have walked many, many miles these last few days and nights, for when I arrived at Katunga's village you had already left. If you will come and help us to destroy this lion the good Lord will reward you and you will make many good friends."

" This lion that you speak of, my friend, how does it come that he carries off a woman and her child so far into the bush in such quick time that your hunters could not track him down before dark? I have never heard of a lion that will carry off two people—even if they are dead. Perhaps the story you are telling me is not true and you are only trying to get me out to your village so that I may shoot meat for you? "

" No, Bwana; I swear that is not true. If I had known you would talk like that I would have brought you some of the bones we found. None of us can understand how this lion carried off two people; perhaps he is a very big animal, and if the child was tied to his mother's back it would not be so difficult, for lions have great strength. It is also true that there was not much daylight left when we went on the trail, and soon after sunset the men all returned home, for they were afraid of the dark. You must believe me, Bwana, and come to help us. If I have lied to you, then you may shoot me with that big gun of yours."

" And this village of yours, how far is it from here? "

" It is *Mbali Kidogo* [a little bit far]. If we leave now and walk fast, we will sleep quite close to it tonight."

Mbali Kidogo is an elastic term I distrusted more than any other in the Swahili language. During the years that vague description had cost me many hundreds of miles of fruitless walking; but it was evident to me that this runner was in earnest and greatly distressed by the thought of my possible refusal to proceed to the ill-fated village.   His story, at all events, carried conviction.

Shortly after this interview our safari was on the way to Mulenga's village, in the Kandoa district of the Belgian Congo.   That night we slept near a water-hole, still " a little bit far " from the village.   We had walked a full twenty miles that day, and Ndege was holding out the most dire threats should it turn out that we had come on a false alarm.

" An escapade like that will get you into trouble with a white man who shoots first and discusses afterwards," he warned the messenger.

" You will see *M'dala* [old man].   If you are not carried off by the lion yourself, you will come back and tell me he is a beast possessed of great cunning and evil," replied the other.

It was shortly after noon the next day that we arrived at Mulenga's village, where a great welcome awaited us. I was soon in conversation with the headman, who repeated all I had heard previously from the messenger, but he had quite a lot more to add to the story, for it appeared that on the morning the runner had left for Katunga's kraal, a party of hunters had trailed the lion and actually caught a glimpse of him, but he was already on the move, and the resulting shots had missed the target.   (With the exception of Ndege, who was an excellent shot on a moving target, I cannot remember ever seeing a native who could be relied upon when shooting at a running animal.)

The natives all agreed that he was an enormous lion. The fact that they had had him under fire must have allayed the fears of the villagers, for the next afternoon an old man and his son were walking home from their plantation;   the old man had fallen back and was sitting under a tree, trying to extract a thorn from his foot, when there was a vicious grunt as the lion claimed yet another victim and disappeared into the bush.

" Yes, Bwana," the son assured me, " he is an enormous beast, and my father must have been killed instantly, for I never heard him utter a sound after the lion sprang on him. I carried only a spear, and I was afraid to follow him into the dense bush."

Again the hunters had gone in pursuit, and again the trail was abandoned at sunset.

For the rest of the afternoon there was but one topic of conversation around my tent—the man-eater and his unbelievable cunning. It was obvious that the villagers were all terrified and at their wits' end, for their best efforts so far had brought no results whatever.

" If he would have attacked in the village like the others did, the trouble would have come to an end long ago," explained Mulenga. " But this devil is so cunning, he never approaches the village, and every time he attacks, it is from a different direction."

What I was listening to was not at all an unusual story, for once a lion resorts to man-eating he operates with extreme caution and cunning, and will evade the best trackers with the greatest ease. What I had to determine here was: did this lion attack only when he was hungry or was he killing for the sheer lust of killing— something very unusual for even the most persistent man-eater. It was quite obvious to me that any attempt to track down this brute would be a very problematical business, and might easily take weeks. There was only one thing to do, and that was to lay down meat baits at night and erect box traps with two compartments and live bait inside.

Goats, of which there were plenty in the village, would answer the purpose best, for they will bleat for hours when left in solitary confinement, away from the herd. I discussed the matter at length with Mulenga and my trackers, and they all approved of my scheme.

Strange as it may seem, the villagers here knew nothing about the construction of box traps. They had on several occasions laid meat traps at night and sat up waiting high in the tree-tops for the marauder. On moonlight nights the lion had scrupulously avoided the bait. On a few occasions he had approached the bait on dark nights, but without spotlights they had failed to get him under fire on these rare occasions. This did not surprise me, and added little to the reputation of cunning of the lion, for from the description of the methods they employed to lay the bait, it was apparent that the meat was placed much too near the trees in which the hunters sat waiting. A lion would have to be ravenously hungry to take bait under such conditions.

Once our plans were decided on and explained to the villagers, a sudden change came over them, for now their conversation was confined not to the havoc the lion had created among them, but to the certainty that, in a day or two, they would celebrate the demise of their arch-enemy. That night the camp-fire burned brightly outside my tent.

Ndege, as usual, had the floor all to himself, and as more beer flowed he related the harrowing detailed accounts of each lion he had seen killed in similar circumstances. I listened to some of the most hair-raising stories ever invented by man. Ndege had many true stories to relate, but he also had a most fertile imagination. It was well past midnight when the last stragglers returned home with Ndege's solemn assurances ringing in their ears.

" Tomorrow night, my friends, I assure you, your troubles will be at an end. ' Congo ' [my nickname] knows just how to handle this situation. Go home and sleep peacefully; you have nothing more to fear."

Ndege had said his piece, and as far as his audience was concerned, a lion-skin would be stretched out under a nearby tree by this time the following night. It was as simple as that! For myself, I did not share any of Ndege's confidence, and I felt certain that, even with a fair share of luck, it would be several nights before his wild assurances were realised.

Under normal conditions a lion can be lured into a trap fairly easily, but a man-eater is a bird of quite different plumage. Once he has taken to this evil habit, he develops a cunning that will strain the resources of the most experienced hunter to the extreme. I had no doubt at all that this cunning brute was going to provide us with lots of trouble and disappointments—to say nothing of danger.

Early the next morning Mulenga and his men were outside my tent, ready for the day's work. I selected two spots in opposite directions some distance from the village where the box traps were to be erected. Abele, my other tracker, was an expert at the task, and I left him in charge whilst Ndege and I, accompanied by twenty men from the village, set out in search of game to provide the necessary meat for bait that night.

Game was by no means plentiful in this area, and it was after 4 p.m. before we returned with two zebra carcasses. I selected two large trees, a mile or so from the village, and on the higher branches of each we laid a rough platform with bush poles. I got the natives to do a " drag " of meat for a mile or so around the trees and left small pieces at short distances to attract the lion to the main baits near the trees. Ndege, armed with a heavy-calibre rifle and a spotlight, would take up his position in the one tree, whilst I took the other. In each of the two box traps a goat was fastened; their bleating could be heard in the distance. Shortly after dark we took up our respective positions in the trees—the stage was set for the night's adventure and hopes ran high in the village.

I had not been in the tree for more than an hour before I became aware of the presence of an animal at the bait, which was securely tied to a big log. I waited until I could hear the bones being crunched before switching on my torch—to find a hyena helping himself to the meat. The moment the beam of light fell on him he made a wild dash into the bush. During the rest of that night there were several more visits from hyenas, but the lion failed to put in an appearance. Ndege had a similar story to tell, but he at least got a glimpse of the lion in the rays of his torch as the brute stood watching a hyena at the bait, but the lion made off before he could get a shot at it.

By morning most of the bait had been consumed by prowling hyenas, at which we could not shoot for fear of frightening away the lion, should he be near by. At the box traps there was another story of failure, for the best result we obtained here was a spotted hyena who sat looking at us from the interior of the cage with an expression of deep misery in his eyes, and lost no time in putting the greatest possible distance between us when we opened the cage door. Around the box traps there were numerous tracks, one set of which, I was convinced, was left by a lion. Apart from providing a good feast for the hyenas, our first night's vigil ended in complete failure, and Ndege's solemn assurances ended in thin smoke.

The next night produced similar results: the lion failed to put in an appearance, and made no sound to indicate his presence. By now our meat supplies were almost exhausted, and after a few hours of sleep in the morning we again set out in search of game to replenish supplies.

Late that afternoon we caught up with a herd of zebras, one of which I bagged, whilst a wounded one disappeared into the bush. We followed the trail for a considerable distance, but by sunset we decided to abandon the trail and return early next morning.

That night, being tired and sleepy, we laid bait at only one tree, which Abele, the other tracker, occupied. Apart from hyenas, no other animal approached the bait that night. The box traps were likewise empty. Up to now we had caught three hyenas in the two traps, but they also were now giving the traps a wide berth.

Early the next morning we were back on the trail of

the wounded zebra. The blood trail led into thick bush and then entered an open clearing. We had just arrived at the half-consumed carcass when Ndege grabbed my arm and whispered:

" There he is under the tree, Bwana."

It was as the lion sprang to his feet, a little more than 100 yards away, that I squeezed the trigger of my heavy-calibre ·425. There was a savage grunt as he leaped into the air and fell down, tossing his huge frame about. My next shot, on an easy target, was a complete miss, and I could not see what the result of Ndege's shot was. In the next instant the lion entered a large patch of green grass. By this time most of the natives had found safety in the tree-tops. This was just as well, for from these vantage points they could watch the open clearing beyond the grass patch.

Half an hour later the lion had failed to emerge from cover; he was either dead or lying in wait. I quickly sent a runner back to camp to call out the villagers for a beat. In little more than an hour they were all on the scene, carrying an assortment of pots, pans, empty tins, drums, spears, pangas and every other instrument of warfare they could lay their hands on. These natives had come there in the firm determination to flush the lion from his hideout, and it was with great difficulty that I could restrain them from starting the beat before the strategic position for the guns was determined.

At the far end of the patch the grass tapered to a narrow point. I decided that Ndege and I would take up our positions at the extreme end of the grass and about twenty yards to the side. I had a hunch that when the pressure was laid on, the lion would try to escape at that point. The natives were instructed to form a crescent and start the beat as soon as I gave the signal. As luck would have it, there was a small tree with outspread branches at the very point where I decided we would take up our positions. As soon as we got into position with our rifles resting on the protruding branches, I whistled loudly. That was the signal for the beat to commence.

In a second, pandemonium reigned around that grass patch, for apart from the pots, pans and drums which they were beating with wild abandon, the natives were chanting a war-song and shouting at the top of their voices. There was not the remotest likelihood that any animal in the African bush would remain long in the vicinity of that din. At the same time the noise made it impossible to hear any slight rustle in the grass. The best Ndege and I could do was to watch closely for any sign of grass being trampled down.

A few seconds later it came at high speed. It was with difficulty that I could train my sights on the moving grass; the lion was running true to form and making as near as possible for the point where I expected him to emerge. Another few seconds and a large black-maned lion streaked into the open. A second after he broke cover I squeezed the trigger, Ndege followed up almost simultaneously, and the big brute rolled over on his side. With two heavy-calibre slugs in his body, there was no question about the result; but for all that, I kept him covered as Ndege went forward to investigate.

" He is dead," shouted Ndege as he stood looking at the big carcass.

I went up and examined the carcass carefully. There were two fresh bleeding wounds, one through the heart, the other through the stomach, but there was no sign of the wound I had inflicted earlier in the day. Inside the patch of grass there was still a great commotion, and the natives were dancing around in a circle and shouting at the top of their voices.

" We've got him, Bwana! We've got him! " they yelled as I approached them.

They were not aware of the fact that we had " got " the other one too at the end of the grass patch. So loud was the noise during the beat, and so intense their concentration on the job on hand, that they had failed to hear the two shots.   For once the great carcass was not riddled with spears, for the beaters left him as they found him, dead, with a ·425 slug through both lungs—an injury from which he must have died shortly after he entered the grass patch.   The other lion had remained next to his dead companion until, too late, he realised his mistake, and walked into two heavy-calibre slugs, fired from a distance of twenty yards.

I could detect no signs of disease in these two lions; both were in very good physical condition and quite capable of running down their prey in the bush.   What, then, is the explanation of two lions in perfect good health resorting to man-eating?   The explanation may lie in the fact that they were bred from man-eating parents, and acquired the taste for human flesh early in life—for human flesh is definitely an acquired taste among the carnivora of the African forest.

That night there were scenes of the wildest excitement among the villagers;   the only thing that dampened their spirits was the fact that the beer brew would not be ready for four days.

" A fine lot you are here in this village," Ndege told the headman.   " We have come all this way and gone to all this trouble to rid you of two man-eating lions who would have devoured you all in good time, and there is not as much as a pot of beer to show your appreciation. Tomorrow ' Congo ' will have the safari on the way again, and by the time your beer is ready for drinking we will be many miles away.   It is a poor reward, my friend, a poor reward indeed."

But on this occasion " Congo " was not quite so heartless.   After all, Ndege was in at the end for the kill, and, seated near the camp-fire with an ample supply of beer, he could again draw on his fertile imagination and tell of some of the most hair-raising adventures that had no foundation in fact.

We stayed for the celebration, and during the next few days I supplied the village with large quantities of game meat. This was going to be the father and mother of all celebrations in the bush.

" We have worked very hard these last few days, Bwana, and at last the beer is ready," announced Ndege on the fourth day. " You are not going to hurry us on the way again before we have finished our celebration? " he queried.

" No, no, Ndege; I will stay until you have had your fill of beer, until it is all over."

A week later I had benefited by the much-needed rest and decided that it was time to get the safari on the way again. My share of the swag was the eternal gratitude of the inhabitants of the village and two beautiful black-maned lion-skins. These I cured and softened and sent to a good friend in America. The gift was appreciated so much that in return he sent me a splendid little ·22 Savage Hornet as a present. It was as a result of the glowing reports I sent back about the performance of the little rifle that I became involved in a long and acrimonious dispute with the editor of a famous American outdoor magazine, and this eventually led to my writing my first book about my adventures in the African bush.

Two days later we were ready to leave.

" Where are we making for now? " queried Ndege as we started to move off.

" For the next bend in the road, Ndege, for the next bend in the road. Who knows what awaits us there? "

CHAPTER VI

MAN'S INHUMANITY

IT WAS SHORTLY after midnight, and my wife and I were sound asleep in an enormous barn which I had turned into a cottage by inserting two extra walls. We were living on the Chongwe River, thirty miles from Lusaka, the capital of Northern Rhodesia, and just on the boundary of a large Native Reserve.

Our cottage was only about twenty yards from a busy main road, and some fifty yards below us lived the native from whom I rented the barn, which he had built with a view to running the place as a dance-hall and tea-room for the passing native trade. I was at the time operating a copper mine near by which kept me fully occupied, employing as I did, some hundred and twenty natives.

This night, like so many others before, saw us in bed by ten o'clock. Now we were rudely awakened by the squealing of pigs, the cackling of fowls, and the blood-curdling screams from my landlord's wife.

"Bwana, Bwana!" she screamed in the direction of my house, "come quickly and help me; there is a wild animal here attacking us."

It was a pitch-black night without moonlight, and earlier in the night several light showers had fallen.

In the eighteen months I had lived in this house I had frequently gone out in search of game, and found the country completely barren. During all that time I had seen only one female duiker. In Northern Rhodesia there are some ten thousand native hunters, all using antiquated old-model muzzle-loaders; it is reliably estimated that they *kill* forty thousand animals each year and wound more than twice that number.

The Chongwe River area, being a Native Reserve, had suffered more from the depredations of native hunters

60

than most other parts. Thus, with the complete absence of game to attract carnivorae, this frantic appeal for help against a prowling animal was puzzling and startling.

As quickly as possible, I lit a hurricane lamp, grabbed my rifle and spotlight, and rushed out to the scene of the trouble. On arrival there the woman showed me her horribly lacerated arm, from which a piece of flesh had been torn. She assured me that " the animal " had actually devoured the flesh and had departed at my approach with the lamp. In an enclosure there were two dead piglets and several dead fowls. " The animal " had certainly caused a lot of destruction in quick time.

" But what kind of an animal was it that caused all this damage? " I asked the woman.

" I do not know, Bwana," she replied. " It could not have been a lion, for had it been I would have been killed. It was not a hyena, for I have seen many of them and I would have recognised it. It may have been a jackal; it stood more than three feet high and attacked me when I tried to drive it away from the fowl-run."

I was completely at a loss to understand just what kind of animal could have been responsible for this carnage. Had it been a lion, the woman would have suffered far more serious injuries than she did. A hyena is the most unlikely animal to attack a human being under such conditions, and no jackal I ever saw stood more than three feet high, and, like hyenas, jackals do not normally develop man-eating tendencies. Still, I had all the evidence of a savage animal's handiwork.

I gave the immediate surroundings a thorough going over with my torchlight, but could not see anything. The tracks of the animal also puzzled me. They were large enough for it to have been a young lion or a hyena, but the woman was most emphatic that it was neither a lion nor a hyena.

I then turned my attention to the woman. She was in a bad way, and in urgent need of medical aid, for the wound was bleeding profusely and she suffered acute pain. I dressed the wound as best I could, and a few minutes later one of my drivers, for whom I had sent urgently, appeared on the scene. The woman was bundled into a car and sent off to the nearest hospital in the Reserve. By this time all the surrounding huts were in an uproar; the cause of the trouble was a puzzle to them, and they feared that at any moment the mysterious animal might return and repeat the attack.

Natives are always afraid of anything they cannot understand or explain. This strange animal who attacked so ruthlessly was completely beyond their understanding, and already there were murmurs about witchcraft and animals possessed with evil spirits. The village medicine man was already on the scene, and after walking around in circles for a while he sat down and shook his head gravely. He had no doubt at all that witchcraft was responsible for the trouble, that it was an animal possessed of the evil spirit, and that it would without doubt return again to wreak further damage. The fear of the unknown and superstitious beliefs in evil spirits that invade the sanctity of human and animal bodies take the form of positive reality with them.

I was not unduly impressed with the medicine man's diagnosis of the case, but, like everyone else, I was completely mystified by the night's events. When I returned to bed after 4 a.m. there was no question of sleep again, for I was not only puzzled but also seriously worried; there was no way of telling when or where the next attack would be. It was quite logical to expect that this mysterious animal, having made one attack, would most likely return again.

Early the next morning I organised a gang of natives to scour the country. Black, my old gun-bearer of hunting days, was handed a rifle and instructed to leave no stone unturned in finding the mysterious creature. The entire countryside was given a thorough going-over that day, but when the gang returned just before sunset it was to report that they had found no trace of the animal.

That night the whole native population went to sleep in a panic of fear, and all doors were securely fastened. I also took similar precautions and remained awake until midnight, in case the mysterious creature should again put in an appearance. I was in a heavy sleep at 3 a.m., when I was awakened by loud screams which came from a hut some 200 yards away. Again I grabbed my rifle and rushed to the hut from whence the screams came.

On arriving there I found the place in great turmoil. In reply to my inquiries I was informed that the mysterious animal had again tried to raid a fowl-run. The occupant of the hut had rushed out with spears, but on seeing him the beast had snarled and disappeared in the dark. He only got a glimpse of the creature, and the two spears he had thrown at it had failed to hit the mark. Like the woman of the previous night, he could give only the vaguest description of the animal. It might have been a lion, but he did not think so. It could have been a hyena, but from the little he could see of the form of the animal he did not think it was. A jackal, also, it might have been, but he had never seen such a big jackal before. A leopard it certainly was not, for he would easily have identified it.

I was back to the position of the previous night. This mysterious animal who would take a lump of flesh from a woman's arm and devour it, come back the very next night and again menace the livestock, had me completely bewildered. The only helpful information the occupant of the hut could give me was that the animal did not dash away quickly, as wild animals usually do when they are disturbed, but had moved off slowly; he was afraid to follow it too closely for fear it might turn on him, and perhaps it was as well that he missed the mark with his two spears, for the beast might easily have turned on him had he wounded it.

As the animal did not dash away hurriedly after it saw the native, there was just a chance that it had not gone far, and I decided to follow in the direction it had taken and try to locate it with my spotlight.

A quarter of an hour later I picked up the two shining eyes in my torchlight. I walked up slowly, carefully holding the eyes in the beam of light. When only about twenty yards separated us I squeezed the trigger. As the bullet struck home the head dropped: there was no doubt about my having placed a brain shot, and I walked up slowly to investigate. The horrible sight I saw there was the most revolting thing I have ever seen in the African bush. The carcass was that of a completely emaciated skeleton of a Great Dane dog. So starved was the animal that no more than three inches separated the stomach from the spinal cord—in fact it was nothing more than a bag of bones covered by skin. That animal had been driven completely insane by the pangs of hunger, and in that desperate state he had made his two last dying efforts to appease his hunger.

It was the old, old story all over again: a well-bred dog, stolen from a European and taken into a Native Reserve many miles away. Great Danes, owing to their size, consume large quantities of food, and must be fed on meat. They take badly to the fare the natives provide for their own dogs. This dog had proved too expensive for his new master to feed, and had therefore been driven away to fend for himself. Untrained in hunting and the ways of the bush, the animal had slowly starved until it had reached its present condition. I shuddered to think of the suffering of that poor beast, who probably came from a home of comfort and was then left in the bush to his own resources.

There have been many occasions during my hunting days when I have stood and looked with great satisfaction on the carcass of a " pot provider " or a killer animal, brought to book, but never have I looked upon a dead animal with so much satisfaction as I did upon this poor hunger-crazed creature, whose body had become so deformed through starvation that even the natives could not identify him as a dog.

The native treatment of dogs in every territory in Central Africa is a revolting crime against nature. In many cases they have not sufficient food for themselves, owing to their laziness and indolence, yet they will breed dogs by the score and leave them to scavenge food for themselves. The brutality does not end there, for whereas a native will very rarely beat his child—no matter how serious the offence—he will subject a starving dog to the most heartless brutal beating for stealing a mouthful of food. I can vouch for many dogs having been beaten to death for such an offence.

CHAPTER VII

FUN WITH THE KING OF BEASTS

It was towards the end of March that each member of the European staff of the Red Locust Control Organisation in the Rift Valley received a circular letter saying that the campaign, but for one or two small areas, had terminated, and every Control Officer was requested to proceed to a little native village named Kalumbaleza with his labourers and equipment, where it was hoped to disband the entire force " in the near future ".

By the time I reached Kalumbaleza, which is one of several small villages on the edge of the Valley and over-shadowed by a range of mountains, the name of which I have now forgotten, some fifteen Europeans and several thousand natives had already congregated at the spot. In view of the fact that during the latter part of the campaign the supply organisation had failed completely owing to the heavy rains, this senseless idea of bringing some five thousand men to an isolated point well off the main supply routes was a sure way of asking for serious trouble, and trouble we did encounter at a very early stage.

It was intended to disband the force within a few days, but we remained at Kalumbaleza for over a month before the first move towards dispersing the force was made. By this time most of the available food supplies were completely exhausted, and the situation to a large extent resolved itself into a struggle for the survival of the fittest.

In a very short time hygienic conditions at Kalumbaleza became completely intolerable, and I saw more flies there in an hour than I had seen in fifty years before. Flies, unfortunately, did not provide the only unpleasantness, for there were many other evil factors at work. Soon hunger was stalking the land, and the few chickens, goats, and sheep to be procured from the surrounding villages were quickly devoured. Maize was quite unobtainable. This new army of " two-legged locusts " had, in fact, laid the country barer than any swarm of locusts could ever have done.

Hunting offered but slight relief, for as a result of six months' Control activities in the Valley, the animals in the area had been widely scattered, and native hunters on the fringes of the Valley had, as usual, taken their toll of game.

In the Control Organisation there were only three South Africans who had had any previous experience in hunting, and they were armed with old ·303 model Service rifles—only a step or two ahead of the bow and arrow. None of the other European staff had ever done any hunting before and they could therefore not be relied upon to help in any way.

Among them was a little Greek who had bought himself an excellent double ·600 Jeffery elephant gun, for which he paid seventy-five pounds at a sale. During the campaign he had never had occasion to use the rifle, and it was on the day I took him out that he fired his first shot from it. Immediately he had squeezed the trigger the gun went flying in one direction, whilst the Greek was deposited on the soft part of his anatomy five yards from where he had fired the shot.

" Is this thing intended to kill the animal one shoots at or the man who fires it? " he queried as he pulled himself together and offered me the rifle for one-tenth of its value.

In my own case, I did not fare too badly, for along with Black and one or two others of my old hunting crew, I went out on daily excursions, and had moderate luck in keeping my own entourage reasonably well supplied with meat. It was hard going, and often involved long marches through dense grass and swampy marshes.

Still, there is no incentive like an empty stomach to stir a man into some sort of activity, and hunting at the moment was the one and only activity that helped to keep the wolf from the door, so we persisted at it. In this manner we survived the ordeal better than most of the other members of the organisation.

At Kalumbaleza village the old headman, Mulopi, had a herd of over twenty cattle, which he kept in a kraal at nights. Mulopi, like most other natives in Central Africa, would not part with any of his cattle, even for cash offers far in excess of their actual value. This is a strange trait with natives which I have encountered throughout my life in the bush. Often I have come to villages during bad seasons where natives were literally starving to death, whilst their kraals would be well stocked with goats, sheep and cattle—as hungry as themselves—but it would never occur to them to kill off their livestock for their own sustenance. If an animal died from starvation or as the result of an accident, they would all gather around the bag of skin and bones and gorge themselves. This reluctance to part with livestock is often extended even to fowls and eggs.

Mulopi was a native of this type, and his possessions in livestock made him an important member of the local community. The tax man presented him with no worries, for he had three sons who had joined up in the locust campaign, and the money they brought back would amply provide for all his immediate cash requirements. We of the Locust Control Staff could all starve to death if we could find no other way out of the difficulty. His cattle were not for sale, and that was all there was to it.

It was after the villagers had all retired one night and Mulopi must have been dreaming dreams of affluence and avarice that fate struck him a particularly cruel blow. That night his cattle kraal was raided by a lion, who killed two of his oxen and departed with a half-grown calf. This happened on a black, moonless night and during a heavy drizzle. The savage snarling of the lion and the bellowing of the cattle stampeding in all directions were clearly audible to us all in our camp, and Mulopi had an even better audition, for his hut was only about fifty yards from the kraal. Possessed of only an old muzzle-loader and no suitable lighting equipment to serve him in the circumstances, he had wisely decided to stay indoors and leave the lion alone.

Early the next morning there was a great commotion in the village. Two oxen lay dead in the kraal, whilst not more than a hundred yards away were the few remains of the calf which the lion had carried off. Mulopi was greatly distressed at this terrible misfortune which had befallen him, and the situation was not improved when he found that the best offer he could get for the surplus meat was a little more than a penny per pound. His inconsiderate treatment of the few European members of the staff did not gain him much sympathy from that quarter, and when he came round later in the morning to appeal for help, he had a rather frigid reception from the few members who normally might have taken the chance to sit up and wait for a raiding lion at night.

At that time I was many miles out on the plain looking for game, and it was shortly before sunset that I got back to camp. That day had been a particularly good one, for I had managed to bag a zebra and a fine big roan bull. For some days at least the food situation would be eased. After a quick bath and clean-up I returned to the tree where the two carcasses were being dissected. There I found Black and Mulopi in earnest conversation. I had a pretty good idea as to why Mulopi had chosen that moment to be present on the job, and was not anxious to give him an opportunity to open a conversation which I knew would end in an appeal for help. But keeping within earshot, I could hear the trend of the conversation between the two.

Black was now holding forth in a voice especially

intended for my benefit. " Last night's business, my friend, was definitely *shauri ya Mungu* [the Will of God]. You are not so foolish as to believe that the bwana is going to interfere in such a matter? " he said. " For two weeks you have watched people here almost starve to death and you have refused to help by selling even as much as one fowl. I have been present night after night when men have prayed for the good Lord to punish you for your wickedness, and their prayers are being answered. Not only will the lions kill all your cattle, but in the end they will kill you as well. You have brought all this trouble on yourself, and my advice to you is to go to the big boss and sell your cattle to him before the lions kill the lot."

Mulopi was deeply impressed by this speech and sat shaking his head for a while, but, unlike Black, he was not prepared to believe that the situation was entirely beyond all cure. For him there appeared to be a better and more practical solution to the problem, and in a few seconds he knelt before me, clapping his hands in an appealing gesture. He was most apologetic and regretted his hardness of heart in the past. He was, in fact, quite willing to dispose of a few head of cattle in order to help out, if in turn I would help him to curb the lion's activities.

" As things are now I will have no cattle to sell in a very few days' time, for I lost five last night—three killed and two others that have disappeared completely."

Mulopi's misfortunes did not disturb me unduly; his off-hand manner and indifference to our troubles during the two previous weeks had antagonised me as they had everyone else, and I could not care less if the lion killed all his cattle in one night or in one week. But the thrill of curbing the evil ways of a raiding lion is an inducement that no serious hunter will turn down lightly. When Mulopi left me half an hour later he had my promise that I would do my best to help him out of the difficulty.

That night there was no further trouble, and early the next morning one of the stray oxen was found standing near the enclosure. Later in the day the remains of the other ox were found a little more than a mile from the village. The carcass was cleaned to the bone and bore all the traces of the handiwork of hyenas and jackals after the lion had taken his share.

With two kills to his credit in such a short time, I did not expect the lion to raid the kraal again in a hurry. Meanwhile I managed to persuade two members of the Control Staff to take a hand in curbing the brute. In the next two days the kraal was heavily reinforced, and we left only a small section through which the lion could easily force his way, should he return—it is not true that a lion can jump over a ten-feet-high fence with a bullock in its jaws! In addition to the extra protection around the kraal, I got the natives to erect two observation posts, which we camouflaged skilfully. One post would be occupied by my two companions, whilst Black and I would occupy the other. Four days had elapsed since the raid, and that night found us all at our posts, each doing an hour's watch whilst the other slept, but the night passed without incident.

The following night we were back at our posts, each taking his turn at watching. It was whilst I was having my forty winks shortly after 3 a.m. that Black jerked me by the shoulder, but before I could switch on my shooting-lamp a shot rang out from the other post. There was a vicious grunt and a rustle in the grass as the lion disappeared in the dark. The excitement for that night, at least, was over. The loud grunt after the shot was fired indicated that some damage had been done. If the wound was not serious enough to kill, it was quite certain that the lion would not return to that locality for a long time—or at least until hunger forced him to do so.

Early the next morning we examined the position in daylight. The tracks showed clearly that a front paw had been struck, and for a mile or so it had bled freely. The trail then entered the open plain, and we left it at that. The excitement, as far as Mulopi's kraal was concerned, was over, and we called off the night watches.

For the next ten days I went out regularly in search of game and managed to keep one step ahead of the wolf. Then, late one afternoon, we came across a herd of zebra. With the critical food situation in camp, I prayed fervently that I would be lucky enough to bag one with each round in my magazine. But the zebras had different ideas and kept on the move. When I finally opened up the range was close on 300 yards. My first shot was luckily well placed and had an immediate result. The animals fortunately panicked and grouped together; I dropped another, and a third was badly wounded and followed the herd. It was a mile or so before we picked him up in a cluster of grass near a big tree.

The porters I had brought with me that morning were barely sufficient to carry back two of the animals. The first two carcasses were quickly dissected and sent back to camp some eight miles away. From there a guide was to bring back a fresh gang to collect the rest of the meat whilst Black and I remained behind to protect the last carcass from hyenas. Profiting from a previous experience which had landed me in serious trouble with a lion at night when I had no lighting equipment, I had on this occasion brought my shooting-lamp with me. If all went well the porters should be back by midnight and all three carcasses would be safely delivered by 3 a.m.

Shortly after 10 p.m. a cold wind sprang up. I was about to start a fire when we heard a loud grunt in the distance; the sound was familiar, and we both made for the tree, which was only about fifteen yards away. Here we sat high up in the branches and awaited further developments. Nearer and nearer came the grunts, and then all was silent for a while. Then, suddenly, there was a vicious snarl as the lion jumped on to the carcass of the zebra. I had meanwhile adjusted my shooting-lamp, and waited for a few seconds to make sure that the lion was actually feeding. It must have been a tasty morsel he had in his mouth when I switched on the light, for as he stood looking in our direction with a menacing scowl on his face, I squeezed the trigger. As the bullet struck home he slumped over the carcass and lay dead.

We quickly descended the tree to examine the trophy. There was no doubt: it was our old friend from Mulopi's kraal. The wound in his front paw was healing slowly, but it must have proved a great handicap to him in hunting his food. His condition showed plainly that he had suffered many foodless days since that night he ran into trouble at Mulopi's village. Finding a zebra all stretched out ready for dinner must have made a great appeal to him, and explains his reluctance to move from the carcass when I turned the light on him. With three zebras, and a lion for good measure, the day's hunting had proved very successful, but the night's excitement was not yet over. With the dead lion covering almost the entire carcass of the zebra, the situation offered the prospect of excellent amusement.

We quickly manœuvred the lion into a most realistic position astride the zebra. A pronged fork was driven into the ribs of the zebra and the lion's head lifted on to it. A large piece of meat was forced down the throat and a thin stick helped to keep the jaws wide apart. The ensemble provided the most realistic terrifying spectacle of a lion lying on its prey. It was now close on midnight, and Black and I returned to the tree-top and sat waiting for the porters to come back. Shortly before 1 a.m. we could hear them shouting and talking loudly in the distance. Occasionally they would light a flare fashioned from dry grass, for it was a dark, moonless night.

" We have arrived at last," shouted the guide as they neared the tree. " I recognise the place by this tree. The zebra is lying in the grass over there. The bwana must be asleep by now. Bring some dry grass so that we may light our way," he continued as they grouped near the two carcasses.

A second later the flare was burning brightly as they proceeded to the spot. Then suddenly the silence of the night was rent by some of the most blood-curdling human screams I have ever heard as the gang vanished into space. By the time Black and I could recover from our laughter they must have been more than a mile away, for there was no response to our calls and the two shots I fired. It was an excellent joke, but in scheming it out I had omitted to foresee the possibility of having the entire gang disappear for the remainder of the night, and Black and I were forced to spend the rest of the night in the tree.

Shortly before sunrise next morning I sent Black off to the camp to bring out another gang of porters and anything eatable or drinkable. In little more than an hour after he had left I could hear voices in the distance. The gang of the previous night had run all the way back to camp and spread an alarming report of what they had seen that night. Accompanied by two Europeans, they had set off at daybreak to come out and collect what was left of us!

Another occasion when lion was not the quarry, but provided the night's entertainment, was when my old friend, Charlie Goss, the elephant-hunter, and I were hunting far down in the Usanga plains in Tanganyika. This particular part of the plain is covered by a deep layer of very fine silt—probably of volcanic origin. We had had a trying but successful day, and returned to camp just before sunset. It was too late to move to the nearest water-hole, ten miles away, as the proceeds of the day's hunt had still to be brought in. We decided, therefore, to stay there for the night and move off early next morning.

Our tents were erected side by side on what appeared to be the only spot where the pegs could be driven into solid earth. When the job was finally completed most

of the guy-ropes of the two tents were overlapping in a
bewildering maze. It was after dark before the first
loads of meat arrived and after ten o'clock before the last
stragglers came in. The natives were all thirsty and
utterly fatigued, for in that part of the plain the temperature frequently rises to 120° in the shade during the
hottest part of the day. Thus, when the meat was
dumped a few yards in front of our tents, we accepted
the situation in order to avoid putting more strain on
the weary porters. The entire hunting staff, in any case,
had erected a rough grass shelter and prepared their
beds only a few yards from the meat-pile and could be
depended upon to keep prowling hyenas away.

It was a few hours before daybreak that one of the
natives became aware of a disturbance at the meat-pile
and, believing it to be a hyena, he lit a grass flare and
rushed out, spear in hand. It turned out, however,
that the raider was not a hyena, but a huge male lion,
who lost no time in vacating the scene. In his hurried
departure he rushed through what appeared to be an
opening between the two tents, and here he got himself
thoroughly entangled with the guy-ropes. The next
instant my tent collapsed on top of me, whilst only a few
feet away the lion snarled viciously as he tried to dis-
entangle himself. The whole incident could not have
lasted much more than five seconds, for when Charlie,
now thoroughly awakened, rushed out with rifle and
torch in hand, the lion had already departed.

After it was all over everybody laughed heartily at
what they considered a very good joke, but there was
mighty little for me to laugh at when I found myself
buried under a tent with a lion standing snarling
menacingly only a few feet from me!

Sitting in the lounge of the Chunya Hotel on the Lupa
Goldfield in Tanganyika one night, we hunters and

diggers discussed current topics pertaining mainly to hunting and alluvial digging. It was just before midnight when a friend of mine, " Windy " Coals, decided it was time to get back to camp. " Windy " was never a hunter of any importance, and although he always carried a little ·22 Savage Hornet, which he could use with deadly effect, his interest in hunting extended only to providing for the pot. A few minutes after bidding us good night, his motor-cycle could be heard roaring out a staccato roar as he took off.

Half an hour later we had all gathered on the front veranda prior to retiring for the night when " Windy " came roaring back at full speed. His face was as white as a sheet as he related his story. Riding along at a moderate speed and watching out for any stray buck in the rays of his shooting-lamp, he had picked up a pair of eyes of an animal standing in the main road. It was one of those cases where ignorance is bliss, and " Windy " felt certain it was a hyena. He had stopped the motor-cycle, lined the eyes up in his sights, and squeezed the trigger. He had then walked over casually to examine the trophy, and was almost jerked out of his skin when he discovered that it was not a hyena, but a huge male lion. This had happened not much more than a mile from the little township, and we all went out to verify the story. It was indeed an excellent trophy, and the only mark on the enormous carcass was the missing left eye where the bullet had entered.

This lucky escape unfortunately ended up in tragedy for " Windy ", for he now felt convinced that shooting lions was no more difficult or dangerous than shootng duikers. In putting this theory to the test in Uganda less than a year later, he ran into serious trouble when he followed a wounded lion into close bush. The lion had attacked unexpectedly and subjected him to such a terrific mauling that he died a few hours later.

CHAPTER VIII

ENEMIES OF SOCIETY

Now that I have severed all relationships with the bush and settled down to town life, friends often ask me what possible pleasure there can be in a life in the wilds, with its dangers, insecurity, lack of comfort and un-settled conditions. To those who have lived in cities all their lives and grown accustomed to the comforts and amenities of town life, it must seem strange that there are people who find contentment and distraction in an existence which, for the greater part, fails to provide even the elementary necessities they consider so essential to human welfare.

To the average lover of nature, animals, from the elephant down to the tiny bush-baby, and birds, from the ostrich down to the honey-sucker, are a source of enthralling interest and delight; but when it comes to the insect world—in which I include the scorpion, the locust, the tsetse-fly, the spirilum tick, the jigger flea, the mango fly, the tarantula, the centipede, the raider ant and the mosquito—I agree they can make life exceedingly unpleasant.

The scientific study of these insects, I have no doubt, is a very interesting subject, but to be compelled to have them as room-mates or bed-fellows is quite a different matter. I have often wondered just what useful func-tion, apart from making life intolerable for the hunter, these creatures perform in the scheme of nature. During my many years of wandering in the African bush I have had many unpleasant encounters with these enemies of society, but whenever an opportunity presented itself I found it interesting to study their habits—from a distance—in order to try to find some explanation as to the reason for their existence. The question, to a large extent, still remains unanswered.

It was not my interest in the life and habits of the tsetse-fly that induced me to make weekly trips through what I believe is the worst tsetse-infected area in Africa, and that was a fifteen-mile stretch near the Uruwira Mission in Tanganyika.   Seated in the back of an open vanette, I would pass my hand over my back at intervals of five minutes, and it was seldom that I collected less than twenty tsetses.   A fairly large percentage of flies in this area were infectious, and during the twelve months I operated in this part of the country there were over seventy cases of sleeping sickness, including three fathers of the White Fathers Mission.   Just why I never contracted the disease is something I will never understand, but what was nearly as bad as the disease itself was the daily dread that the last bite might bring about a dose of sleeping sickness in ten days' time, and every headache was a sure indication that an attack was imminent. This kind of existence can be very trying, and I was very happy indeed when, a fortnight after I had left the district, I was still free of the disease.

The abundance of tsetse in this stretch of country raises an interesting point, for it is generally claimed that the tsetse-fly depends entirely on blood for its existence, and it is for this reason that more than a million game animals have been destroyed in the interest of tsetse control.   In this fifteen-mile stretch of country near Uruwira Mission I never on any one single occasion encountered any game animal of any description.   If tsetse-flies depend on blood in order to live, I have often wondered how the ten million flies in this area eke out an existence?

Although I have, in the course of years, destroyed many hundreds of head of game on tsetse control, the experience at Uruwira has raised the gravest doubts in my mind as to the wisdom of such measures.   Most of the vast open plains in Central Africa teem with game, yet I have never encountered a tsetse-fly in these open spaces; on the other hand, the forest country surrounding the plains is generally heavily infected with fly. I do not dispute the fact that blood is a valuable adjunct to the diet of the tsetse, but I am convinced that, even if all the game in Africa is destroyed, the fly will remain as active as it is today. The remedy is not the indiscriminate destruction yearly of thousands upon thousands of game animals. Why is it that the Society for the Protection of Game in Central Africa does not put up a more determined fight against this senseless destruction of game but meekly accepts the dictum of legislators who are obviously floundering in the dark?

That the average city-dweller should have an exaggerated fear of insects and reptiles is quite understandable; it is due mainly to the fact that they rarely come in contact with such creatures and are, therefore, ignorant of their ways. In my wanderings in the bush I have found that natives who are in daily contact with snakes, lizards and insects, are even more afraid of them than the conventional city-dweller. I have yet to meet the native in the wilds who is not convinced that there is no cure against the bite of a harmless chameleon, and that in spite of the fact that the chameleon has no teeth with which to bite!

When I pushed a chameleon down the back of a porter who was sitting near the camp-fire one night, he turned white, and demanded his pay the next day. Whenever I wanted to be left alone and free from the thousand and one worries of my native staff, all I had to do was to allow a few pet chameleons to settle on my head or shoulders. To their way of thinking there is only one harmless chameleon, and that is a dead one.

I spent many hours in the bush lecturing natives about their evil habit of killing harmless creatures, and always emphasised the fact that every living creature has a useful function to perform in the scheme of nature. This assurance always puzzled them, and I was often hard put to justify my statements. When Black, my old gun-bearer, sat down on a log one night and received a painful sting from a scorpion on the soft part of his anatomy, he immediately posed the question to me:

" What good do these creatures ever do in this big scheme that you are always telling us about? "

I had to think up an answer to that one very quickly, and succeeded in convincing him that the scorpion had rendered him an excellent service, and that was to teach him to be careful and examine logs before sitting down on them in the dark.

" Had it been a poisonous snake instead of a scorpion, you would have had a lot more to complain about," I concluded.

Black sat down and thought things over carefully for some minutes and agreed that there was some logic in my argument. " It is true, Bwana, that fellow has taught me to be more careful in future, but is that the only work they ever do? "

I did not think it would be wise to go deeper into the question, for natives are very much like children, and they will often ask questions that cannot be answered without reference to text-books. I may, of course, have told him that scorpions form a very important part of the diet of baboons and monkeys, and that the apes have made a far better study of them than most natives, for natives all believe that scorpions can bite as well as sting, and as in the case of the chameleon, there is no cure against the *bite* of a scorpion; the *sting* is painful, but one gets over it, the bite is fatal in every case. The apes have no such illusions. When I kept twenty-seven vervets in an enormous cage, most of the compound kids were out daily searching for scorpions, which I bought from them. Whenever I threw a tinful into the cage there would be a rush for a share in the spoils, but the scorpions would be approached with studied care. To watch these little apes, or baboons, for that matter, giving a scorpion the works is a lesson in dexterity. The head is quickly pushed into the ground, and as the tail curls up preparatory to a sting it is neatly nipped off between the thumb and forefinger; after that the scorpion is devoured at leisure without the slightest fear of a bite.

I have often seen it written that scorpions will commit suicide by stinging themselves to death when angered or threatened; this in fact is scientifically vouched for in some text-books. Whereas I am not prepared to dispute this claim, it is a fact that on dozens of occasions I have enclosed a nest of scorpions in a ring of fire and brought the fire closer and closer until it must have been very uncomfortably hot, but on no single occasion did I ever see a scorpion sting itself. The man in Moscow takes a glass of vodka for sundowner, the man in Glasgow prefers Scotch—it is simply a matter of habit—and it is quite possible that the scorpions I watched had not yet acquired the habit of stinging themselves to death. Perhaps the scientists are on safer ground when they tell us that scorpions inhabited the earth some thirty million years ago and that they have not changed materially during all those years.

So far as I am personally concerned, I have no serious quarrel with scorpions, for in all the years in the bush I was never stung by one of them; that experience awaited me until I had returned to city life in Rhodesia and discarded the habit of shaking my clothes and shoes carefully before dressing in the mornings. I was introduced to the business end of the tail of a scorpion that had crawled up my trousers leg during the night, and before I could dislodge the brute he had inflicted three painful stings in my leg. *A la* Jack Dempsey, who attributed his defeat to the fact that he " forgot to duck ", my trouble was due to the fact that I " forgot to shake ".

The red locust is another pest which I was able to study carefully during the six months I spent as a Control

F

Officer in the Lake Rukwa area.   It was here that I met Professor Uvaroff, the world's greatest authority on locusts.   It was Professor Uvaroff who, after many years of painstaking work, determined the breeding habits of the migratory locust and made it possible to attack and destroy the evil at its source by killing the hoppers in their breeding centres before they reached the flying stage.   It is many years since swarms fifty miles long and five miles wide were last seen in Africa, and the swarm that passed over the Red Sea in 1899, which covered over 2,000 square miles and was estimated to weigh over 42,850 million tons, could have been largely prevented if more had been known at the time about their breeding habits.

In the Lake Rukwa area—perhaps the worst breeding centre in Africa—I often destroyed concentrations that consisted of many millions of hoppers.   I was only one of twenty-five Control Officers who sent in daily reports of such large concentrations.   The fact that all these concentrations were destroyed before they reached the flying stage speaks volumes for the present-day control measures.   When one takes into consideration the fact that each female locust deposits on an average one hundred eggs, it is easy to understand how such vast swarms are formed.   Once a swarm of red locusts has taken to the wing, it is capable of flying up to 1,200 miles without alighting.   The locust is one of the few creatures on earth who can comfortably eat his own weight of food every day.

Present-day control measures have gone a long way towards preventing large swarms from leaving the breeding areas, but they are unfortunately not the final answer to the question, for locusts easily build up a certain immunity against the poisons used for their destruction.   A very serious handicap to control work also is the fact that egg-laying, incubation, and the five stages of development before flight all occur during a period of three months in the midst of the rainy season, and to spend three months in the marshy swamps of Lake Rukwa and Lake Mweru with rain pouring down day and night is not exactly my idea of a picnic. For some reason it never occurred to Black to ask me to explain just what function the red locust fills in the scheme of nature, for if he had, I would not have known which text-book to refer to for the answer.

But, for all that, it was possible to live in close proximity to swarms of locusts without suffering any direct ill-effects. The same could not be said of the spirilum tick—one of the most loathsome of all African insects, which is responsible for spirilum fever, commonly known as tick fever. Only those who have suffered from a severe attack of spirilum fever can give an accurate description of what a bad headache really feels like. And that is not the only inconvenience, for if the disease is not checked in time it generally leaves the victim blind or paralysed.

On one property where I worked just before the last war, we were compelled to burn down a compound of over four hundred huts because of the spread of the pest. At one stage more than half our labour force was affected, and after the compound was reduced to ashes the entire area had to be fenced off with barbed wire to prevent natives from squatting there, for burning is no cure against a spirilum tick; they find their way deep down in the crevices of the ground, where they are not affected by heat.

The quickest and surest way of collecting a dose of spirilum fever is to sleep in old, abandoned native huts. There have been hundreds of nights that I have sat out in pouring rain near an abandoned hut, knowing full well that the worst a bad drenching can do for one is to bring about discomfort and, perhaps, a bad cold; both are easily overcome—a dose of spirilum fever may take years to get rid of, and may often leave one with a form of facial paralysis and even blindness. As in the case of the locust, I have never been able to determine the role of the spirilum tick in the scheme of nature, and as in the case of the locust, I have never discouraged natives from killing them. There are very few hunters in Central Africa who have been lucky enough to escape the attention of these insects—I was one of the lucky ones.

Then there are the jigger fleas and mango flies, which have but one function in the great scheme of nature, and that is to make life truly miserable for man and beast. The jigger deposits its eggs under the toe- or finger-nails, and once the egg is deposited, there is only one thing to do, and that is to wait patiently for ten days or so until it has multiplied itself a thousand-fold and is ready to burst the containing sac. Most natives are skilful in digging the sac out whole, but if by chance it is ruptured in the process, the movement starts all over again in a much-aggravated form. I have seen many natives with most of their toes completely eaten away by the friendly jigger.

The mango fly operates on a similar pattern, but on a much larger scale, for it will deposit eggs indiscriminately on clothes left out to dry. Each egg develops into a worm from a quarter to half an inch long, which digs itself into the body of its victim. A well-known Johannesburg engineer called at my house one night and complained that he was suffering from a severe body rash. It took me over two hours to extract seventy-three worms from different parts of his body. It was lucky for him that we had access to adequate supplies of disinfectants and antiseptics to prevent the sores from turning septic.

I had my full share of suffering from the friendly attentions of these unwelcome pests. So did the last lion I ever shot, for this unfortunate creature had fallen foul of a porcupine, who left several broken quills in his jaws and paws, and in these open sores the mango flies had speedily deposited hundreds of eggs. At the time of our meeting, Leo was all but starved to death and must have been suffering the greatest agony from the numerous festering sores. The ·333 slug which I placed in his brain must have come as a welcome relief to him. " These devils do not even wait until one is dead before they start eating," remarked Black as we examined the carcass of the lion.

Centipedes also are among the most dangerous and unpleasant of forest pests. Just why they are so called I do not know, for the most legs I ever counted on a full-grown specimen amounted to twenty-eight. They are especially numerous during the rainy season, and often find their way into one's bed-clothes. When a centipede fastens his tentacles into one, it spells trouble with a capital T, for each point carries a powerful dose of virulent poison, which, if not promptly attended to, will turn gangrenous. My acquaintance with these loathsome creatures never extended beyond a quick-killing act.

I consider one of the greatest of all Central African pests the red, or raider ant. It is strange, but true, that the elephant, the world's largest land animal, will flee from a column of one of the smallest insects—the raider ant—and the elephant is not exactly an animal that will panic without cause. I have spent many hundreds of hours watching these murderous little devils at work, and could easily fill a volume in describing their handiwork.

One of the worst hard-luck stories of the bush concerned a hunter who spent several months in the Kivu Mountains on the trail of gorillas. He was hunting on behalf of a well-known American society, and after months of negotiation he was finally granted a licence by the Belgian Government to capture baby gorillas on a fifty-fifty basis, i.e. half his catch had to be handed over to the Belgian Government.

After a nerve- and health-wrecking venture which lasted more than three months, during which time he lost over five stones in weight and narrowly escaped death on half a dozen occasions, he finally left the Kivu with four baby gorillas. On the third or fourth night of his return journey the gorillas were safely covered up in their cages and left near his tent for the night. When he went out next morning to attend to them he was horrified to find that one cage contained only the completely denuded skeleton of a gorilla—a column of raider ants had passed that way during the night. On his way back to Europe he lost two more gorillas, and finally landed in Brussels with only one—which the Belgian Government promptly claimed.

One of the most unpleasant camps for insects and reptiles I ever occupied was on the Chongwe River in Northern Rhodesia. Accustomed as I was to the bush in the raw, I found the conditions there extremely trying. For my wife, who was a newcomer to the bush and who had spent all her life in cities, it was a nightmare experience. One night, a few days after her arrival, we were sitting listening to gramophone records when she drew my attention to a movement on the floor quite close to her. I quickly went over to investigate.

" Nothing to worry about; it's only a type of earthworm we have in these parts," I said as I put my foot on the creature.

Nearby there were four more of the same kind of " worms ", which I quickly killed. In actual fact they were baby cobras, and I made a thorough search of the place in case there were others. I did not expect to find the mother of this brood in the immediate vicinity, for snakes are a little lax in the matter of parental responsibilities and usually leave their offspring to fend for themselves from the moment of birth. But in the case of cobras these unpleasant little devils are born with a near lethal dose of poison in their fangs. Two hours after birth they can kill a fowl, and at the ripe old age of twenty-four hours they are capable of inflicting a fatal bite on a human being. It was for this reason that I was anxious to make sure there were no others about.

During the fortnight preceding the arrival of my wife,

I had kept a gang of natives busy clearing the entire area around the house; all boxes, bags, or other possible hiding-places were carefully inspected, and the clean-up yielded a splendid collection of cobras and puff-adders. I felt reasonably certain that there were no others left in the vicinity, but this mother cobra must have found her way up into the rafters during the clean-up. Just what happened to her and the rest of her brood I never did find out. Cobras are somewhat prolific and generally give birth to anything between thirty and sixty babies.

A few nights later there was yet another disturbance, when an enormous ball of brown fluff suddenly deposited itself in the centre of the room. Closer examination revealed it to be a monster-size tarantula—the largest of its kind I have ever seen. I had no ready explanation to offer, nor could I dismiss this horrible creature as perfectly harmless, as I did the dozens of hunting spiders that frequented the place. Apart from their hideous appearance and the speed at which they move about, these are really quite harmless, and I have never heard of anyone being bitten by a hunting spider. They are, in fact, useful creatures to have in camp, for they prey on the smaller insects that are harmful to man. But most women object to them on account of their gruesome appearance. My wife was no exception to the rule.

I was having a difficult time belittling the obvious dangers and unpleasantness of our unwelcome guests when one more misfortune befell us, and that was when a column of raider ants awoke us from sleep one night. Huge masses of ants hung all over the rafters and poles of the building, whilst a steady stream of millions passed through the roof. In my anxiety to do something helpful, I foolishly interfered with the formation of the column; instead of making them change direction, as I had hoped, the column scattered, and in a few minutes the entire house was alive with ants. It was several hours later before the column had again re-formed and went on their way in an orderly fashion, leaving us unmolested.

It was still necessary for me to do something that appeared practical to safeguard us from any stray members, and to this end I hastily filled four basins with water, in which the legs of our bed were submerged. I was fully aware of the fact that this was no protection against the ants, for if they were so minded they would speedily build a bridge with their own bodies. My assurance that we were perfectly safe, however, had the desired effect.

Pushkin, the pet ape, was similarly " protected "—his cage was mounted on a table, the legs of which were also submerged in dishes of water. That column of ants must have consisted of many millions, for it was fully six inches wide, and their march through the house lasted for over sixty hours. It was a nerve-wrecking business living and sleeping in a house through which a continuous stream of ants passed for more than two days. At one stage of its advance the column attacked a nest of field-mice; in less than half an hour only the bleached skeletons remained.

A few nights later yet another column passed through our native compound and drove the occupants from their huts. Black, justifiably infuriated after spending a night in the open whilst the ants made merry in his hut, was there early the next morning to pose the question: " What is their function in this great scheme you told us about? "

At the time he was busy cleaning and scraping a pair of buffalo skulls for me, a job he thoroughly disliked and which normally would have taken him several days.

" Bring those skulls along, and you will see how useful ants can be," I told him.

The skulls were duly deposited in the path of the column, and we left to attend to current daily work; when we returned in the afternoon the ants had disappeared, the two skulls were thoroughly and properly cleaned, without a trace of brains or flesh remaining. Black stood looking at the skulls for a while, shook his head, "You white people, you know everything," he muttered as he walked off to his hut.

Last, but not least, there is the mosquito. There are very few people living in Africa who have not, at one time or another, made the acquaintance of this pest. In the Rift Valley, whilst on Locust Control, I saw not only the largest cobras in Africa, but also the largest mosquitoes. Luckily they were not infectious, and apart from forcing us under the mosquito nets shortly after sunset every day, they did no serious damage. This was different from the Belgian Congo in the early days, for there repeated doses of malaria inevitably led to blackwater fever, one of the most deadly of all tropical diseases.

I was standing talking to a friend of mine one night whilst the doctor was busy inside attending to his wife, who had contracted blackwater. Her condition was extremely grave, and when the doctor emerged from the room he informed the husband that there was nothing more he could do and he did not think she would survive the night. My friend was naturally greatly distressed, and I did all I could to try to comfort him in the circumstances.

It was whilst I stood talking to him that an old native from a nearby village appeared at the door. I knew the old man well, and he explained to me that the reason for his sudden appearance was to tell us that he was certain that he could cure the memsahib if she was still able to swallow a mixture he would prepare quickly. He had brought along a supply of roots from a tree which grew in the vicinity, and these were to be boiled in water and the resulting brew taken at frequent intervals. Neither of us had much confidence in the old man's assurances, but in such a desperate situation one tries everything and hopes for the best. For the rest of that night we gave her repeated doses of the brew; the next morning there were distinct signs of improvement, a week later she was out of danger, and after that she made a rapid and complete recovery.   I used those roots with success in two other bad cases of blackwater subsequently, and was never without them in the bush after that.

In these days, with several highly effective anti-malarial cures on the market, blackwater is seldom, if ever, heard of, and no one will ever think of resorting to native roots for a cure, but this is 1957.

CHAPTER IX

JUNGLE WOMEN

THE JUNGLE IS a place for men—men who are able
to adapt themselves to its requirements, who can take
the ups and downs, the hardships and insecurity with a
smile and find compensation in the thrills, the excitement and the adventure it offers. In my own case, I
have always found the compensations more than adequate, and that is the reason why I, like so many others,
have preferred the life of the bush to that of the city.
But it has always puzzled me to find that there are
women who have a similar outlook on life; women who
find happiness and contentment in a life that surely was
never intended for the opposite sex.

It is true that in these emancipated days of equality
of the sexes, women often successfully invade what was
previously the stronghold of the male sex, and for the
greater part the situation is accepted as perfectly natural
and normal. But that they should successfully emulate
the men of the bush and find the same happiness and
contentment there, strikes me as something very extra-
ordinary, and I can find nothing but praise and admira-
tion for those women whom I have met in this strange
and unnatural setting.

It was in my very early days in the Belgian Congo
that I met the first of these strange women. At the time
of our meeting she had recently settled down on a piece
of land she had acquired, some forty miles from the
nearest small village. She was then living by herself
in a little log cabin, and employed thirty native labourers,
who were busily engaged clearing and ploughing her
land. Quite close to her cabin was an enormous bush
enclosure, the walls of which were some fifteen feet high
and as many feet wide, and provided shelter for her

donkeys and other livestock at night. This was very necessary, for she was living deep in the forest and in bad lion country.

As I stood talking to her, my attention was drawn to a huge lion-skin which was spiked out in the shade of a large tree. She offered the information that the " big fellow " had given her a lot of trouble and that she had spent a full week on his trail before she finally brought him to book. The surprised look on my face must have prompted her to add that she had accounted for several others during the past few months, but they had not given her much trouble, as she had picked them off with a shooting-lamp at night whilst they were trying to raid her livestock. Assuming that she was living there with her husband, I suggested that she must have held the shooting-lamp whilst her husband did the shooting.

" Oh, no," she replied, " my husband has been dead these past fifteen months; I shot all four quite close to the enclosure; it is quite easy at night." A few moments later she proudly displayed the four skins hanging in a little store-room near the cabin.

Further conversation revealed that this woman, in her late forties, of good appearance, fair-haired, and somewhat frail in build, had come to that part of the country to settle down and cultivate the land. It was right at the beginning of the development days of the Union Miniere, the vast copper-mining company in the Belgian Congo. She felt that, with the rapid expansion of the Company and the prospects of large numbers of Europeans and natives soon to be employed, the little town would grow rapidly and provide her with a steady market for her produce—maize, potatoes, vegetables, etc.

" For the moment I am under-staffed, for it is not easy to come by the necessary foodstuffs to provide for a big gang of natives. I go out as often as I can spare the time, but game is not plentiful here, and the best I can do is a couple of antelopes a week. Just before the rains set in it was much easier, for the buffaloes came to drink regularly at the water-pool, and I had no difficulty in keeping the pot supplied with meat; now there is water all over, and they seldom come this way to drink," she said.

Our conversation led to hunting and guns, and I was surprised to find that the heaviest weapon in her armoury was a light 8-mm. German Mauser, a rifle heavy enough to provide for the pot, but certainly no weapon to depend on when dealing with such dangerous animals as lion and buffalo. My suggestion that she equip herself with something more reliable for dangerous hunting was turned down on the grounds that the lighter rifle was easier to handle and " if you hit them in the right spot, they go down just the same ". In several outings with this astonishing woman she provided me with ample proof that she was quite capable of " hitting them in the right spot ", for she was an excellent shot and not in the least excitable.

My activities in the mining and hunting business during the next six years enabled me to visit her farm at fairly frequent intervals; during those years that part of the Congo had expanded rapidly, and, as she had foreseen, there was a persistent demand for her produce, and the little farm prospered. At one time she employed over a hundred native labourers, whom she managed with the greatest efficiency, listening to their many matrimonial troubles, settling tribal disputes, attending to complaints, and allocating the work to the different sections.

It was at that time that I left for the Back Congo on a long safari, and when I called on her again several months later, I was surprised to see a great difference in her appearance, for she had lost weight tremendously, looked aged and haggard, and was obviously seriously ill. She told me that she had been ill for several weeks and that the local doctor, who called on her at infrequent intervals, did not seem to be able to help her very much. With some difficulty I managed to persuade her to accompany me to Elisabethville, 100 miles away, in order to have a proper examination and treatment.

It was on our trip down that she spoke to me for the first time about her domestic and family affairs. She was born in London, and came out to South Africa with her husband, where they lived for a couple of years and then migrated to the Congo. Here her husband had contracted blackwater fever, from which he died two years after their arrival in the country. She had a son, whom she had not seen for ten years, for he was then studying at the Royal School of Mines as an engineer. It was in order to provide him with the necessary education that she had decided to remain in the Congo and develop the property she had bought after her husband's death.

In Elisabethville her trouble was soon diagnosed— cancer of the stomach. Against medical advice, she refused to be hospitalised immediately, but returned to her farm for another two months to put things in order and hand over to a temporary foreman. The son, who was then sitting his final exams, was notified immediately, and arrived in the Congo a few weeks before her death.

Unlike his mother, he had no interest in farming, and the bush did not appeal to him in any way. After her death the property was sold, and he left for Johannesburg, where he set up as a consulting engineer. Just before his departure he called on me one afternoon and handed me the little rifle—in accordance with his mother's wish. I kept the little gun for many years, and on the rare occasions when I used it, my mind always went back to the brave woman, alone in the bush, who depended on it for her protection and safety.

I first met Kathie in the Congo when she was a little girl of twelve years of age. Eight years later I met her again in Tanganyika on the Lupa Gold-field. She was then on her own, running a gang of fifty native labourers on what I consider was at the time one of the world's hardest and most precarious jobs—alluvial digging.

The Lupa in those days was completely primitive, for there was no hospital, doctor, chemist, post office, hotel or any other essential public service. It was a hard life, wandering from one place to another in search of the elusive yellow metal. But Kathie held her own against the toughest of diggers, and whereas most of the men—including myself—were at times in dire trouble with labourers over their pay on account of the irregular and sometimes long delays between lucrative strikes, Kathie seemed to have " a nose for gold " and weathered the storms comfortably.

When finally the field became too problematical, she secured a fishing concession on Lake Rukwa. Here, for some years, she managed the business on her own, and did quite well. The part of Lake Rukwa where she had her concession was one of the wildest in Tanganyika, for wild animals, from crocodiles to elephants, regularly frequented the shores of the lake at this point.

On the one night I spent at her camp, lions were roaring lustily quite close by, but this was a nightly occurrence and did not disturb her in the least, and she did not consider it necessary to have any firearms for her protection. At a later stage she became Game Warden for the Lake Rukwa Game Reserve, and managed the job very efficiently—so efficiently, in fact, that she landed me with the one and only spot of bother I ever had with any Game Department.

The six months I spent as a Control Officer on the Red Locust Staff in the Rift Valley was by far and away the hardest six months I ever spent in any part of Central

Africa. This was during the rainy season, and the Valley was, for the greater part, flooded most of the time. The tour of my area was usually completed knee-deep in water and for much of the time it rained incessantly night and day. Mosquitoes, like locusts, are among the most prolific breeders on earth and helped to make life quite unbearable.

I was sitting in my tent one afternoon whilst the heavens poured more water, when a native messenger handed me a letter from the Chief Control Officer. The letter instructed me to have my camp and labour staff ready for inspection by Dr. L., the Chief Medical Officer of the campaign, who would visit my post on the following Sunday. I was sitting down to dinner on the Saturday evening, whilst outside yet another storm was raging, when a woman's voice suddenly called out at the tent door:

" May I come in? "

Completely startled, I rushed for the door and opened it. Outside stood a woman in heavy overcoat and top boots.

" I am Doctor L., the Chief Medical Officer; my porters are busy erecting my tent out there, and I would love to have a cup of warm tea or coffee whilst I wait."

For a moment I stood speechless, and wondered whether my senses were playing me false. On a night such as this the hardiest of men would think twice before going out in the open at the mercy of the elements and in the kind of country we occupied. Still, there it was, my unexpected visitor was certainly no apparition, for she was again talking busily. I immediately invited her in and had hot coffee prepared.

She explained that the storm had worked up so suddenly that she was caught unexpectedly a mile from my camp, and rather than spend the night standing against a tree, she had decided to make for my camp, where it was possible to pitch tent, the rest of the area being completely under water.

"On the Katavi Plains I bagged two or three buffalo bulls daily"

"That big bull is not only a killer and a raider . . ."

"My share of the swag was eternal gratitude and two beautiful skins"

"The food situation was improved when I bagged three zebras that day"

A crocodile in the interminable swamps off Lake Rukwa where Kathie had her concussion

"He went down near a big palm tree"

"The larger animals are usually hunted by prides consisting of two or more members"

"The scavengers are always waiting for the king of beasts to vacate the scene"—a jackal at a lion's kill

A pride of eight at the kill. At this stage the cubs are not allowed to approach

(*Above*) The wild dog mother regurgitates to feed her young

(*Left*) "The baby was quickly taken from the wounded mother"

"Hippos have the pools to themselves during the breeding season and the croc is *persona non grata*"

"Cheetahs are the most wasteful of hunters"

(*Left*) African witch doctors—the switches in their right hands are used to ward off evil spirits

(*Below*) A camp scene in Northern Rhodesia

The doctor remained for dinner, and left for her tent in pouring rain just before midnight. The following day the inspection was carried out according to schedule, and later in the day she was on her way again to the next camp. In the distance dark clouds were once more banking up, and I wondered to myself just how she would fare before she reached her destination.

My camp was only one of many she had to inspect over a distance of some hundred miles, and the entire personnel—white and black—exceeded five thousand in number. During the six months I remained in the Valley she visited my camp quite frequently, and as far as I know the service was maintained on a very high standard of efficiency under the most appalling conditions. Just how often she was forced to plod in heavy rain and mud at night whilst doing her rounds I do not know, but it is quite certain that the conditions under which she worked never interfered with her good nature and cheerfulness, for whenever she visited my post there was always a genial smile and a keen desire to be helpful in every possible way.

Long after I left the Valley I heard she was still on the job and doing well. What courage and determination a woman must possess to plod through those interminable marshes near Lake Rukwa at all hours of the day and night, in a mosquito-ridden country, and where every other poisonous insect and reptile may be encountered at any moment! The hardiest of men would not contemplate such an undertaking without suitable firearms for protection. This amazing woman never carried anything more formidable than a walking-stick to make walking easier in the mud.

There was the lady, the wife of a famous big-game hunter who I met in the Valley of Death in the most

G

peculiar circumstances, which I have described elsewhere. For ten years she shared the life of the bush with
one of the most restless of all hunters, for his activities
took them to almost every Central African territory,
including Angola, Kivu and Ituri forests in the Congo,
Uganda, Sudan, Kenya and Tanganyika. She herself
had been an actress on the English stage, and came out
to Africa in order to settle down to jungle life with her
husband.

Some years after our meeting her husband was killed
in an automobile accident in New York, where he was
busy negotiating with a cinematograph company to send
out a team to film his exploits. After the death of her
husband she returned to the life of the bush, and soon
she had his old staff of hunting-boys back on the job.
At one time she was carrying out a government control
job on the border of Tanganyika and Northern Rhodesia;
this involved considerable elephant- and buffalo-shoot-
ing, but she seemed to manage quite well on her own.

Shortly before I left Tanganyika I received a letter
from her enclosing a photo of two fine male lions she had
accounted for. " I was lucky this time," she wrote,
" for I got the two in two shots with my heavy ·404
rifle." She did not mention anything about the range
or the conditions, but that is not of great importance; to
bring down two lions in two shots is a man-size job,
whatever the conditions.

Perhaps the most remarkable woman I ever met in the
bush was a German lady. Her story was strange and
unique. At the beginning of the last war she and her
husband were farming in the Ufipa country in Tanganyika, where they had been for many years and qualified
as residents. At the outbreak of hostilities they promptly
reported to the nearest District Commissioner and swore

allegiance to the British Throne and were allowed to return to their farming operations without hindrance.

Then, when Hitler had overrun the greater part of Western Europe and was knocking at the gates of Alexandria in Northern Africa, the husband suddenly had a change of heart, and with a " Heil Hitler " he advised the District Commissioner of the fact. He was immediately taken care of and sent to an internment camp. The wife, however, did not share his sentiments, and she was allowed to continue the farming operations under strict government control.

Under the existing conditions she was deprived of all arms and ammunition, and had to report regularly at the nearest administrative post. For the rest, she was left to fend for herself as best she could. The farm consisted of many thousand acres, and was stocked with some two thousand head of cattle, large numbers of pigs, goats, sheep, etc. There was a meat-canning factory in operation, and a large part of the farm was under maize and vegetable cultivation.

For the rest of the duration of the war she took sole charge, and managed this vast undertaking with her native labourers. I first met her when I was on safari, shooting meat for a mining company. She landed at my camp late one afternoon with a herd of two hundred cattle which she had sold to the Company. It is true there was very little femininity in her appearance. Dressed in man's attire, standing fully six feet tall, hands hard and calloused, hair closely cropped, and shod in a pair of heavy top boots, it was only the fact that she introduced herself as Madam D. that made me realise that she was a woman, and not one of the hardy male adventurers one occasionally meets in those parts.

Our conversation around the camp-fire that night was casual, and confined to local current affairs and the progress of the war. I listened with interest when she spoke of her many activities on the farm. She, in turn, was interested in hunting and inquired about my

progress.   Of personal hunting experiences she had very
little to tell, for in that part of the Ufipa where she was
farming there was no game at all, except for the occasional lion or leopard.   In any case, she had no firearms
for hunting, and therefore had nothing of interest to
tell.   We did not have a great deal in common, and
shortly after dinner she retired to her tent for the night.

Soon after she had left the camp-fire, Black, my old
gun-bearer, was at my side.

" Bwana, is she really a woman? " he queried.

" She does not look very much like a woman," I
replied, " but she is the lady who runs the big farm up
in the Ufipa country."

" Did she tell you about the leopards? " he queried.

" No," I replied.   " What about the leopards?   She
never mentioned anything else except that there are
some in her part of the country."

" Wait, Bwana, I will call her herdsmen over here to
tell you about it.   If what they say is true, then she is
not a woman, but five men rolled into one."

A few moments later four of her herdsmen were seated
around the fire and Black urged them to tell me the
story.

" There is nothing much to tell," said the leader of the
quartette.   " On the farm where we come from there
are lots of leopards, and we have a great deal of trouble
with them, for they come often to raid the livestock at
night.   The memsahib has no guns, and with the help
of her dogs she goes after them with a chopper when
they come too near the place.   She has killed several
during the past twelve months since I have been there,
and she has lost two of her best dogs in that time."

" Do you mean to tell me that, with the help of a few
dogs and an axe, she follows leopards at night and kills
them single-handed? " I asked.

" That is just what she does, Bwana.   You see, there
are no trees for the leopards to climb, and the dogs are
well trained.   There are at least a dozen of them, and

they are all bigger than a leopard. They are not afraid of leopards, and as soon as the trouble starts the memsahib comes out with a torch and an axe. The dogs are much faster than any leopard, and quickly surround him. As soon as the memsahib comes on the scene they attack. She stands close by, and the moment she gets the opportunity she hits the leopard over the head with the chopper. It is a big chopper and very sharp. One hit is enough; it just opens the skull. The memsahib is very strong—much stronger than any of us—and she is not afraid."

That, then, was the incredible story that Black had found so hard to believe, and for my part I was even more sceptical. Shortly after daybreak the next morning we were all sitting round the camp-fire again waiting for early morning coffee. The leopard story I had listened to the previous evening was uppermost in my mind, and I immediately got on to the subject and asked the lady about it.

" Oh, yes," she replied, " I have killed a few that way. The natives make an awful fuss about it, but there really is not very much to it. You see, I have an excellent breed of lion-dog and they are not afraid of the lion—or leopard, for that matter. The most difficult part of the job is to get in quickly when the dogs attack and before the leopard is able to get on his back, for then it is difficult to get at him, and often he does great damage with his claws. I have lost a number of good dogs that way and others have been badly mauled. The right time to swing the axe is when one of them gets hold of the leopard by his throat and the others fasten on to his body. They will hang on grimly until I can get busy. One good hit is generally enough."

The story seemed so incredible that for a moment I was lost for words and sat looking at her.

" You do not seem to be convinced by what I have told you," she said. " If you are interested, I have three or four skins at home, and they will bear out my story.

If you wish to buy them, you may have them for five pounds each. They are all undamaged except for the mark on the heads where the axe landed."

Without more ado I booked all the skins she had on hand, and these she promised to send on to me at the first opportunity. Three weeks later a passing motorist left a grain-bag for me at the property. Inside were three leopard skins; each bore evidence that the skull had been split by a sharp instrument—undoubtedly the chopper I was told about. In a covering letter the lady explained that she had one more skin left, but it was rather badly damaged, as she had had a " spot of bother " and did not kill with the first stroke. Just what, I wonder, could have happened when she had that " spot of bother " in the dark with a leopard at bay?

I am a great lover of leopards in captivity and have kept them as pets for many years, but I also know that they are one of the most dangerous animals in the African bush, and nothing on earth will persuade me to go into action against a leopard with a chopper at night when he is fighting for his life—dogs or no dogs. What is more, I doubt if there is a hunter living anywhere who will take such a chance. A similar story, with a man in the leading role, would be hard enough to believe; for a woman to fill that role seems completely incredible. But I must believe it, for apart from what she told me and the testimony of her natives, I had the indisputable proof of the three skins with the axe-marks on their skulls to convince me.

There is an old saying to the effect that " if you stay long enough the bush will eventually catch up with you ". In the case of my friend, she played her luck right through until the end without untoward incidents. But when the bush eventually caught up with her, the setting was rather tragic, and must have left a deeper scar than any leopard ever succeeded in inflicting upon her.

During all this time, and in fact for two years after the war, whilst she played a lone hand on her farm, her only daughter was away at college in the South. After she had completed her education she returned to the farm, and there she met a young friend of mine. Within a year they were married, and the mother's wedding gift to the couple was a valuable farm which she had bought for them. For a couple of years they worked hard, and the farm had reached production stage when the young husband had the misfortune to walk on to a cobra and was bitten in the leg. They were many miles away from the nearest doctor and lacked the knowledge or experience to deal with such an emergency, and a few hours after the accident the husband passed away.

CHAPTER X

JUNGLE LAW

IT WAS AT a time when I was fully occupied with other work and had no time for hunting that I received an urgent appeal from another mining company to come out and try my luck with a lion that was causing a lot of trouble. The property was some sixty miles from my camp and employed over one hundred Europeans and some two thousand five hundred natives. At the time of writing to me, the lion had confined his attentions to livestock and dogs—something very unusual for lions. As in the case of man-eating, a lion has to be desperately hungry before he will eat any member of the dog family, and that includes hyenas, jackals and wild dogs. In this particular case it was feared that when the supply of dogs was exhausted the raider would devote his attentions to human beings.

I was not particularly anxious to accept this assignment, knowing as I did that when a lion takes to raiding human habitations and enclosures where livestock is kept it is quite impossible to anticipate his movements. To deal successfully with such a situation may require a great deal of time and the unpleasant job of sitting out in the open for many nights without results. In the present case the property was spread over a distance of more than two miles and the prospects were not very tempting. It was after I had received a second appeal that I decided to go out and see what I could do to curb the brute. By this time his visits had become almost nightly occurrences, and both European and native dogs were supplying his daily needs.

I decided to go out one week-end and stay a couple of days. On arriving at the property I immediately laid meat traps, but at the end of four days I had not caught as much as a glimpse of the lion. During that time he had paid three visits to different parts of the property, and on one occasion he had actually jumped on the back of a truck and carried off a valuable watch-dog that was tied up there for safety. The owner had rushed out with a shotgun and fired a shot at the lion as he disappeared in the dark with the dog in his jaws. Some of the pellets must have hit the mark, for the lion grunted loudly as the shot was fired.

The frequent visits of the marauder had so terrified the Europeans that most of them had secured shotguns, which they fired at the slightest provocation. Several natives in the two large compounds were similarly provided with shotguns, which they fired at frequent intervals without reason; but in spite of this fiery barrage of lead, the lion successfully evaded all their efforts to lay him low. This hot reception must have proved too much for the brute in the end and induced him to turn his attentions elsewhere. " Elsewhere " was a small alluvial camp on a river, not far from the mining property, which was operated by a hardy old Boer Afrikaner. Here the lion soon accounted for the few dogs in the camp, and it was not very long before he entered on the next phase of his depredations—man-eating.

Alluvial camps are very seldom of a permanent nature, and huts, for the greater part, are built only to provide shelter against the sun and rain. After the supply of dogs had become exhausted Leo decided to make up the deficiency in his meat supplies by raiding the native huts and carrying off the occupants.

During the first week of his new reign of terror he carried off two natives, and the few who had not departed for safer areas lived in nightly terror of the raider. It was whilst he was sitting in his hut, reading by the light of a hurricane lamp one night, that an old prospector became aware of a scratching and pushing at the grass wall of his shack. He quickly grabbed his shotgun and awaited further developments. A few seconds later

a large hole appeared in the wall quite close to him, and
in the next instant a huge male lion began forcing his
way through the opening.   It was an easy target at five
feet range, and the old man promptly served the intruder with two barrels of buckshot and brought its man-
eating career to an end.

Subsequent examination of the dead animal showed
that it was in fairly good condition;   there were no
signs of disease or injury.   His well-worn fangs indicated
that he was no longer in the first flush of youth, but there
was no apparent reason why this lion, obviously quite
capable of hunting down its prey in the forest, should
have taken to the evil habit of raiding domestic quarters
and finally to the most evil habit of all—man-eating.
The explanation for such perversity in the king of beasts
is quite beyond me.

It was during my unsuccessful visit to the mine that I
met an American engineer who had been on the property for nearly three years.   During that time he had
joined hunting parties almost every week-end, and on
three occasions he had taken part in more important
safaris of several weeks' duration.   In these hunts he had
been successful, in that he shot most of the animals
common to that part of the country, the notable excep-
tions being elephant and lion.   The first and only lion
he had seen outside a zoo or menagerie was the one that
was killed by the old prospector as related above.   Before
long I again resumed my week-end outings, and my
American friend, who was not only a keen hunter but
also a very keen observer, regularly joined me on these
occasions.

Sitting around the camp-fire one night, he posed the
question: " How do you explain the fact that as late as
the end of the last century almost the entire buffalo

population of Central and East Africa was wiped out by rinderpest, and today you can find vast herds of buffalo—in some cases exceeding a thousand head—in many parts of the country?

" During my stay in Africa I have seen at least forty such large herds, but on no single occasion have I ever seen a buffalo cow with more than one calf trailing behind her. By contrast, the lioness on occasions gives birth to as many as four cubs, and seldom less than two. The buffalo is hunted extensively for food by Europeans and natives in every part of the country, and thousands are destroyed yearly by Tsetse Control Officers. The lion, a more prolific breeder, and hunted only for sport or on the rare occasions when he becomes a menace, seems to be a dying race, for whereas I have seen several thousands of buffalo in various parts of the country, the only lion I have seen so far was a dead one? "

My friend had touched on a subject which, at first, puzzled me as much as it did him, and during the many years in the bush I devoted a great deal of time to finding the answer; with this in view, I spent hundreds of hours watching lions in their natural state, and in the end I think I found the explanation. In all those years I do not think I shot more than eighteen or twenty lions, and they were killed for the greater part when, on account of their behaviour, they had placed themselves on the " wanted " list. Watching and studying their habits in the bush whenever an opportunity offered provided me with far more pleasure and satisfaction than killing them.

The lion, the noble creature of the story-books, of the zoo and the menagerie, or even of the protected game reserves where his food supply is ample and regular, is a vastly different animal from the jungle type who is strictly subjected to the law of the survival of the fittest. Strange as it may seem, the lion, with all his physical attributes to conform to this law, strangely lacks the mental equipment to help him in this struggle, and there are many quaint misconceptions about his conduct that will not stand up to close investigation.

The largest of the African carnivorae and essentially a flesh-eater, it follows that he requires large quantities of meat to appease his hunger. It is generally believed that the average adult lion requires at least one or two big antelopes per week to satisfy his needs. This, I am convinced, is a very much over-estimated figure. I feel certain that one large antelope, weighing from 400 to 450 lb., will keep an adult male lion comfortably supplied for a fortnight—all the more reason why lions should increase more rapidly than they do. But with the king of beasts it is not a question of pulling down an antelope once a fortnight and being fully provided with meat for that length of time. Even whilst he is at the kill he is surrounded by scavengers who are anxiously waiting for the moment when he will vacate the scene.

That is the first difficulty he has to contend with in the matter of providing for the future. But there are many other factors that upset the balance. First, the lion is by no means as prolific a breeder as my friend imagined. It is extremely rare for a lioness to produce cubs at intervals of less than two years, and this only when conditions are bad for the antelopes on which they prey. In seasons of drought antelopes generally congregate in areas where water and grazing are adequate. When this happens the carnivorae come in for a good time and breeding is more frequent. But it only requires a slight change in conditions for game to scatter over wide areas; water and food are plentiful everywhere and there is no need for them to concentrate in restricted areas where they easily fall victim to their enemies. To this extent, then, the difficulties of securing their regular supply of food are increased for carnivorous animals, especially the lion, who rarely hunts single-handed, but often in prides of more than ten animals.

So much for the physical problems. On the mental—

or psychological—side, the obstacles against prolific breeding are startling indeed. The lion, as we all know, is a member of the cat family, but in his habits he follows the dog family to the smallest detail. Thus, when cubs are born in a season of plenty, the lioness will provide for them until they are able to look after themselves. The cubs are taught to hunt until they reach the age of eighteen months or two years, and when game is plentiful they soon fend for themselves successfully. But in Central Africa the seasons are fairly regular and droughts are not very frequent. Game is widely scattered and ever on the move. Until such time as the cubs begin to join in hunting parties they are well supplied with food by mother lioness, for she is a good and conscientious provider and will bring back adequate portions of meat from the hunt; she will even regurgitate in order to satisfy their demands. From the age of about two years, however, they are left to fend for themselves.

They will join up with the pride to which the mother belongs, and this pride may consist of anything up to twenty members. They have now entered the dangerous, the killing phase, for a pride may often have to hunt for a full week before they succeed in pulling down something worthwhile. During that week the cubs have had to follow their elders for anything up to 200 miles. They are hungry, worn out, and the strain has proved a great ordeal to them.

Then, suddenly, the luck changes; a large antelope, or even a buffalo bull, is pulled down and there is a determined rush for the spoils; the law of the survival of the fittest is asserting itself. Father and mother lion have renounced all further responsibilities in the matter of providing for their young, and whilst the parents and other members of the pride are at the kill, the cubs are not allowed to approach until their elders have had their fill; a disregard of this rule by the young very often ends fatally.

If the pride is not a very large one the cubs fare

reasonably well by picking the remains of a carcass. But as often as not there is insufficient to appease the hunger of the adults, and the cubs are left with a mental picture of their elders gorging themselves. In a few hours the relentless search for food is resumed, and the cubs in their emaciated state will follow the trail hopefully. But there is a limit to their endurance, and ere long they are lost by the wayside. They have now to fend for themselves, starve to death or fall victim to the lesser carnivorae and scavengers.

One of the most comical and tragic performances I ever watched in the bush was a young lion stalking an mpala. For several minutes the stalk was carried out according to text-book, but as he got nearer to his intended victim his anxiety to secure the kill proved too much for him; there was a wild rush from twenty yards distance, but by this time the buck was heading in the opposite direction fully fifty yards away. The look of disappointment and the air of complete defeat as the lion stood watching the buck, was a picture of absolute despair.

It was on the Usanga Plains in Tanganyika that I once watched an amazing display of greed and selfishness by the king of beasts. Seated high up in a tree with a pair of powerful binoculars, I saw a pride of them pull down a topi. The pride consisted of six adults and two half-grown cubs. All the six adults fell upon the carcase and started to tear it to pieces. The cubs, in all probability even hungrier than their elders, were quickly on the scene to join in the feast. But father lion did not approve of the idea at all, and they were immediately driven to what he considered was a safe distance. It was a pathetic sight to watch those poor little beasts walking round in a wide circle whilst the grown lions were busy gorging themselves. I was unfortunately too far away to hear anything other than the loud growls and grunts of the adults, but I could well imagine those two starving cubs putting up a pathetic wail for a share of the spoils.

After the adults had taken their fill they strode off unconcernedly and lay down in the shade of a big tree and licked their paws.   Their places at the carcass were immediately taken by the cubs, but it was obvious from the manner in which they circled around the dead animal that there was little left for them.   I gave them a full half-hour to collect what they could for themselves and then fired a shot over their heads.   There was a wild rush for safety by the six adults, and a second later the two cubs were trailing behind in an all-out effort to catch up with them.

On examining the carcass I found it completely stripped to the bone.   Just how long those two cubs could survive such rigid conditions of fatigue and hunger is anybody's guess.   For myself, I felt convinced that unless luck turned the scales in their favour very materially in a short time, they would soon fill the role of the topi and fall victims to a pack of wild dogs or hyenas.

This is but one example of greed and heartlessness to be booked to the account of the king of beasts, but there are worse.   My old friend Charlie Goss, the elephant-hunter, once witnessed an incredible exhibition of meanness on the Lualaba Plains in the Belgian Congo. Charlie was essentially an elephant-hunter, and apart from providing for the pot and looking after his personal safety, he had very little interest in " scrap-hunting ".

Late one afternoon he was sitting high up in a tree watching the different elephant paths that led to a water-hole that was popular with other game.   It is near these isolated water-holes that lions usually lie in wait for their prey.   Charlie was sitting watching a small herd of mpala drinking at the pool when there was a sudden snarling and grunting.   Out of a dozen or more mpalas at the water, the lions, a pride of six, managed to pull down only one ram.   In a few seconds the entire pride was busy tearing the carcass to pieces, growling and snarling viciously all the while.

It was at that moment that a cub of about eighteen months old rushed in to secure his share of the meat. Father lion, however, took violent exception to this intrusion and immediately attacked the cub in a frenzy of rage.   When he returned to the carcass there was very little left, but the cub lay dead where the lion had left it. The remains of the mpala were quickly devoured, after which the big brute turned on what was probably the dead body of his son, and started to devour it.   The rest of the pride, not to be deprived of their share of the spoils, immediately closed in to join him in his horrible cannabilistic feast.   But he apparently did not think that any other member of the pride had any right to a share in the meat, and it was whilst he was busy staging a violent exhibition of disapproval that he had the misfortune of getting himself in the way of a heavy ·475 slug.

" Impossible! incredible! " the reader may say.   But this terrible indictment is well authenticated, for, along with another amazing photo of a mamba and a secretary bird in mortal combat, the picture appeared in the *New York Times*, and netted Charlie fifty guineas.

The two incidents I have described here are by no means unique, and there is no reason to suppose that they are isolated cases of lion depravity.   I have no doubt that many other hunters have observed, and can describe similar scenes, and when one considers that the lion is for the greater part a nocturnal hunter, it is not difficult to imagine how many such tragedies are enacted in the dark, when observation is impossible.   I have listened to many stories of a similar nature by native hunters in Central Africa.   In fact, by them it is considered quite a normal occurrence, and none of them looks upon it as something unusual.

In addition to the dangers that threaten young lions which I have mentioned so far, there is still another which takes a serious toll of life among them, and that is the risks to which they are exposed in attacking dangerous animals such as the roan and sable and other

large antelopes. When an overgrown cub is hungry he
throws all caution to the winds and goes in to get the
kill; it is only in the case of the smaller antelopes that
he is a match for his adversary, and the law of the jungle
makes no allowance for bad judgements. The verdict in
almost every case is death for the weaker.

My observations have led me to the conclusion that
no more than twenty per cent of all lions born ever
reach maturity. Long before they reach adult stage
many come to grief by falling victim to the lesser lights,
the small-time hunters of the forest, the scavengers or the
greed of their own parents.

So much for lions in the adolescent stage. Let us turn
the spotlight on the king of beasts after he has come into
his own and reached the age of maturity—four years
and over.

Popular imagination, based upon story-books, has it
that the lion, the noble, majestic beast, is immune from
attack by any other animal of the forest. This is a fallacy
of the first order. In actual fact a great many lions fall
victim (and pay with their lives after weeks of suffering)
to an animal not much larger than a cane rat—the
porcupine. The lion in fact is immune from attack only
as long as he remains in full possession of all his physical
faculties, but it takes very little to balance the scales
against him. I think I am on safe ground in saying
that the lowly porcupine is responsible for more casualties
among lions than any other single cause. Of the twenty-
odd lions I have killed, at least eight were suffering in an
advanced stage from porcupine trouble.

Porcupine trouble to a lion in places where the mango
fly is prevalent is every bit as serious an affliction as is
cancer to the human being. Every quill-wound is
impregnated with eggs which turn into masses of worms,
hunting becomes impossible, and the victim starves to
death in pain and misery—or falls prey to the lesser
carnivora. One lion I shot was in such a bad state that
it was almost impossible to approach him for the smell

H

of the numerous gangrenous wounds. For some strange reason, female lions seldom commit the indiscretion of attacking a porcupine; it is generally the younger lions that fall victim.

Having reached the age of maturity, there are few other causes to reduce the population. The lion, in his natural haunts in the bush, is unfortunately not the heroic, devil-may-care animal of the story-books. On the contrary, he displays a remarkable lack of courage when it comes to attacking the larger and dangerous beasts that provide his daily food. Animals such as the elephant, rhino, buffalo, hippo and giraffe are rarely attacked single-handed; a pride of two or more will take the risk, and in consequence there are very few fatal accidents to the lion.

Human beings are their next greatest enemy, but I do not believe that the situation is seriously affected by the activities of hunters. The average hunter, unless he goes out especially for lion, will shoot at the first worthwhile trophy he comes across. Fire one shot in an area where lions are active and you will not find one for the rest of the day. Native hunters will never go out to look for trouble with a lion unless it is in order to protect livestock or their own safety against man-eaters.

The two remaining factors are disease and senility. Just how many lions die from illness and what kind of diseases afflict them are not very clear. But a fairly large number do attain old age, and when they do they present a tragic figure. For the king of beasts is then menaced and subjected to attack by the loathsome scavengers of the bush who in normal circumstances would flee in terror from his slightest grunt of disapproval.

In Northern Tanganyika my attention was drawn one morning by loud snarling and growling in the dense forest not far from me. Accompanied by my two trackers and a gun-bearer, I proceeded cautiously in the direction of the disturbance. As we pushed our way through the long grass and scrub we came to an open clearing; in the centre of the clearing one of the great dramas of the forest was unfolding itself, for there a pack of wild dogs, numbering perhaps ten, had surrounded a big male lion and were rushing in, one by one, as opportunity offered, to tear at his flesh. All that was left of the king of beasts to remind one of his former glory was his voice, for as his assailants flew at him he uttered loud menacing growls, and these were followed by feeble strokes of his once-mighty paws which the attackers easily avoided.

Closer and closer the circle of death and destruction was being drawn around him; soon even his voice could no longer be heard, as it was drowned in the loud barking and snarling of the menacing dogs. The struggle obviously could not have lasted many more minutes. It was a pathetic, tense, yet dangerous moment, for in their aggressive mood those dogs were capable of attacking anyone who would dare to interfere with their plans. I had fortunately come out fully armed for any emergency, and my trackers were handed a light and a medium rifle each whilst the gun-bearer stuck to the shotgun.

I instructed them to wait until I counted three and went into action with a heavy ·404. The four shots rang out almost simultaneously, and two dogs went down. The rest of the pack, taken completely by surprise, stood glaring in our direction until a second volley accounted for two more. In a flash the others disappeared into the forest, but the lion made no attempt to escape; he was beyond any active movement, and as he stood swaying from side to side I sent a heavy slug through his brain. On examining the carcase I found at least a dozen gaping wounds where the flesh had been torn from his body.

The reason for his lapse into impotence was not difficult to determine. He was definitely in the last stages of senile decay, and his fangs—those deadly fangs which in better days made him the terror of the jungle—

were worn down to grotesque little stumps and could no longer serve him as weapons of offence or of defence. As a consequence, the evil day had come upon him when he, like every other creature of the forest, had to submit to the law of the jungle—the law that provides that only the fittest shall survive.

What an ignoble exit for such a dominating, lordly creature! For despite what I have said to his detriment, the lion is, and will always be, the dominating character of the forest. I have watched him in all his moods, and there is no memory of the jungle that ever made a deeper impression on my mind than the day when I wounded a prize specimen in open country.

For a few hundred yards he ran at fair speed, making for a patch of heavy scrub nearly 1,000 yards away. Half-way to cover he reached a big tree, and at this point his injury must have proved too much for further effort. As he reached the tree he turned round and stood looking at me for a few seconds and then went into a crouching position. There was no grass or scrub to provide effective cover and I had no difficulty in keeping him in full view as I walked slowly in his direction. When only about seventy-five yards separated us I came to a stop to review the position.

He was then lying on his stomach with his head resting on his front paws, watching me intently. I felt I could still reduce the range with reasonable safety and started walking up slowly. With the head still resting on his paws he suddenly started a deep-throated growling— not unlike the purring of a cat, but magnified a hundred-fold. It was one of the most terrifying, blood-curdling sounds I ever heard in the forest and the peculiar setting lent reality to the scene. A few seconds later the black point of his tail came into evidence, swinging from side to side. Every lion-hunter knows just what that means; it was time to go into action—or else. I wasted no time and called a halt to the proceedings.

My American friend who had listened to a great deal

of what I have said here, was with me on this occasion. When it was all over he said: " From what you have told me, this fellow has no claim to nobility, but he is entitled to a great deal of respect, and I am the first to acknowledge it." In that sentiment I could do nothing else but join him.

CHAPTER XI

JUNGLE LOVE

IF THE LION, the king of beasts, fares so badly and succumbs so frequently to the law of the jungle, it is only natural to assume that the lesser lights are even more vulnerable. In actual fact that does not necessarily follow.

The leopard, the next important member of the cat family in Africa, is very rarely menaced by enemies in the bush and steers clear of any trouble with the porcupine—the lion's greatest and most destructive enemy. Man, undoubtedly, is the leopard's chief enemy, and in view of its predatory habits, a large number are killed yearly in reprisals. Unlike the lion, the leopard easily falls victim to traps and poison. The skin, which is of considerable value and easily disposed of, is another incentive for hunting the spotted cats. The traffic in skins in recent years has been responsible for a tremendous reduction in the leopard population all over Central and East Africa until, too late, the governments of these territories have now put them on the protected list.

Although, when hungry, a leopard will eat almost anything in the meat line—even in the last stages of putrefaction—he never resorts to cannibalism and is certainly no scavenger in the strict sense of the word. Unlike the lioness, mother leopard is far more conscientious and devoted to her young, and they are not subjected to the rigours and hardships endured by lion cubs. Young leopards also have the additional advantage that, at quite an early age, they become expert climbers and are fully capable of looking after themselves when their parents are away seeking for food.

This, in the case of the leopard, is not nearly as

problematic as with the lion, for leopards will prey on anything—from field mice upwards. Their favourite prey is baboons and monkeys, which they catch easily in the trees at night. One of the most fearful dins I ever heard in the forest was in the Sira Mountains in Tanganyika one night when a family of baboons was raided by leopards. For fully an hour the blood-curdling screams of the apes could be heard high up in the mountain, whilst the echoes from the mountain opposite helped to magnify the discordant shrieks of terror.

The leopard's other advantage over the lion is that he will rarely leave any part of a kill to be devoured by scavengers. After taking his fill, the rest of the carcass is usually dragged high up in the branches of a nearby tree, where it is safe and well out of the reach of hyenas and jackals.

Not only is mother leopard a better and more consistent provider for her young than a lioness, she is also a better protector. Many lion cubs are captured yearly as a result of being abandoned by their mothers in face of serious danger. The only way you can deprive a leopard of her young is over her dead body, and whereas a lioness will stage a terrifying exhibition of fury in order to keep intruders away from her cubs, the leopard wastes no time on demonstrations. Approach the lair of a leopardess with her young, and it is only a timely bullet in the right place that will save you from a savage mauling.

Of the rest of the carnivora, wild dogs suffer the highest mortality among their young. These animals are ever on the move and cover hundreds of miles during the course of a week. The long absences from their lairs expose the cubs to many dangers, and at best the mothers are poor providers. They generally hunt in packs of anything up to fifty members, and when an animal is pulled down, the carcass is devoured so rapidly that the mothers are hard put to secure a fair share for themselves. Wild dogs are neither scavengers nor cannibals, and depend almost entirely on the meat from the daily hunt.

One of the most fascinating sounds in the bush is their rally call, late in the afternoon. At that hour of the day the forest is generally quiet; suddenly the silence is broken by the call of the leader; this is repeated on several occasions, and from all parts of the forest the scattered members of the pack start to converge to the assembly point, and soon they set out on the trail. They are extremely keen-scented animals and the trail of an animal is seldom lost. Once the victim is spotted there is no escape, for, apart from speed, the wild dog has amazing stamina.

Once the pursuit has started they stick close to their victim, but, contrary to common belief, the pack never attack simultaneously. At frequent intervals during the pursuit a member of the pack will dash forward and tear a piece of flesh from the flanks or legs of the fleeing animal, and it is only a matter of time before fatigue and loss of blood bring the hunt to an end. In a few seconds the entire pack close in on the fallen beast, and it is devoured in a matter of minutes. It is doubtful whether even a lion is capable of inspiring as much terror in animals as a pack of wild dogs; even the fear of human beings pales into insignificance in the face of an attack by these relentless hunters.

This was well demonstrated late one afternoon as I sat in my main camp. The silence of the afternoon was suddenly broken by loud yelping and sounds of hooves coming towards us. A few seconds later a kudu cow with a pack of dogs on her trail came dashing through the bush. She made straight for the veranda of my hut, and there she came to a sudden stop a few yards from me. The dogs, who were close on her heels, were driven off only when a score or more natives rushed from their huts with pangas and spears. One glance at the cow made it obvious that she was at the end of her tether. One of her sides was torn horribly and a hind leg was

almost stripped to the bone.   If she had had the slightest
chance of recovering I should have rewarded her confidence in me by letting her go her way at leisure, but it
was more merciful to put an end to her suffering quickly
with a bullet.

Wild dogs are cowardly creatures and will rarely put
up a fight when cornered.   They have a healthy respect
for man, and whereas it would be dangerous to interfere
with a pack at a kill, I know of no instance where they
have attacked human beings.   The widely held opinion
that they will immediately attack, and devour, one of
their own members if it should be wounded or injured,
appears to be without foundation, for I have watched
several wounded dogs trail along with the pack without
suffering the least aggression.   In cases of extreme
hunger they most probably will resort to cannibalism,
but that holds good with almost every carnivorous animal
—and even with some human beings, for that matter.

The cheetah, another important member of the
African carnivora, is an animal completely apart.   As
in the case of the leopard, man is probably its most
dangerous enemy.   Like the leopard, cheetahs are extremely good providers and their cubs receive a great
deal of care and attention.   They are taught hunting at
a very early age and are never left to their own resources
until they are quite capable of fending for themselves.
Cheetahs hunt in pairs as a rule, and there is always
sufficient left of a kill to take back to their young.
Taking their fill, and carrying back a good share for
their cubs, seem to be their sole interest in hunting, for
unlike either the lion or the leopard, they will seldom
return to a carcass for a second helping.   In this respect
they are extremely wasteful hunters.   Their amazing
speed, dexterity in stalking and the tenacious, bulldog-
like grip at the throat of a victim, place them high on the
list of successful hunters, and for that reason the young
are not subjected to long spells of hunger.   I have not
come across cases of cannibalism among them, but they

rate high among the dirtiest of feeders, and no other animal is so slovenly in the matter of dissecting a carcass.

Hyenas, last of the important carnivora, have always puzzled me. To watch these scavengers at the left-over portion of a kill makes one wonder if they ever think of providing for their young. Since they exist for the greater part on bones of carcasses, it is difficult to understand just how well a few-months-old cub will fare with the massive bones of one of the larger antelopes. Still, they must be reasonably well fed, for hyenas are extremely numerous in Central and East Africa. They are rarely killed by hunters, European or native, and none of the other beasts of prey will go out of their way to feed on a hyena. Lions, in fact, have a positive dislike for the meat of any of the dog or cat family.

Watching these scavengers raid a meat-bait at night, although extremely annoying, has often provided me with good entertainment. Shortly after dark a call will be heard in the distance, and there is an immediate response in another part of the forest. The calls are repeated until they come quite close to the bait, then all is silent for a while. Then a dark, slinking form will emerge from the bush and come quite close to the bait— only to rush back into the bush at high speed for no apparent reason. This is repeated on two or three more occasions, and all is silent for a time. Then a stealthy form creeps up to the bait, there is a sudden rush, and he departs with a good helping of meat in his jaws. Back in the bush he immediately becomes the object of interest of all the others in the vicinity, who will now proceed to set up the most unearthly din to be heard in the forest.

The loud wailing cries are often alternated by hideous, eerie laughter, and this continues until another daring member will return for a helping. This time the raider remains at the bait, where he is speedily joined by the others. The meat is devoured in a few seconds and one by one they depart from the scene. A few minutes later a shrill call is heard in the distance and there is an immediate response from another direction. Perhaps they have picked up the scent of something else, perhaps they are telling me that they have enjoyed the feast I have so thoughtfully provided. Quite apart from helping them to appease their hunger, they have also enjoyed the benefits of a social gathering, for it is only at feeding and mating times that they ever come together; for the rest of the time they live lonely, solitary lives.

Among the non-carnivorous animals, only the largest species will make any serious attempt to protect their young and they are not confronted with the problems of providing for their offspring, apart from suckling the young. There is probably no more dangerous animal in the forest than a mother elephant who believes that the safety of her calf is threatened. Her feelings in the matter are scrupulously respected by man and beast alike. I have heard of cases where elephant calves have been killed by lions, but it is an extremely rare occurrence and a feat that can be accomplished only by a large pride.

Hippos always carry their calves on their backs in crocodile-infested waters, and woe betide the croc who may be so ill advised as to molest a calf accompanied by its mother. One snap of those mighty jaws will instantly kill the largest of crocs. Under normal conditions hippos and crocodiles will live together on good terms, then suddenly the crocs will start to vacate the area. This generally happens at the beginning of the breeding season, for mother hippo believes in making quite sure that there will be no incidents to upset the pleasant relationship.

Buffalo, the most valiant fighters in the bush when their safety is threatened, are stupid beasts, and will stampede when a herd is threatened by lions. It is in the ensuing confusion that the calves are easily pulled down.

Every member of the ape family, from the monster

gorilla to the little vervet monkey, will fight to death to protect their young, and here the responsibility is not left to the mothers alone; the males of every species will immediately join the issue with the females when danger threatens.   Without doubt, one of the most terrifying spectacles in the African forest is that of a big male gorilla coming to the rescue of a newly captured baby.   In practically every case the mother is killed before the baby can be captured, and it is when the little one sets up a squeal that father gorilla will go into action without loss of time.   It is only when you have seen a seven-feet monster, weighing up to 500 lb., baring its fangs, beating its enormous chest so that it produces drum-like sounds, and screams at you, mouth wide open, from a distance of five yards, that you begin to realise how really serious the consequences may be if the attack is not stopped in good time.

I have lived through such an experience once, and I will go to no end of trouble to avoid a repetition.   The Pygmy hunters, with a lifelong experience in such matters, will never dream of attempting to capture a gorilla baby without making sure that " the big fellow " is first taken care of effectively.   In the Kivu Forest the natives told me that one of their men once fell victim to a big male.   The man was killed instantly, after which the gorilla proceeded to pull his head from his shoulders with his bare hands.

One of the pluckiest exhibitions of parental affection I ever saw was when I took out a couple of R.A.F. officers on a hunt in Tanganyika.   There, as every-where else, the baboon is on the vermin list, and when we came across a large family, my two companions, who were inclined to be a little trigger happy, immediately went into action.   During the course of some wild shooting, a mother with a baby hanging on to her was badly wounded.   The baboons were all running at top speed to escape from the hail of bullets, when the leader, an enormous male, looked back and noticed the mother in distress. He immediately retraced his steps, and, human like, he stretched out his hand. The baby was quickly handed over to him, and he went on his way with the mother following lamely behind. A few seconds later she collapsed and rolled over, dead.

The little vervets, the most treacherous, and perhaps the most universally disliked of all the ape tribe, have the most deep-rooted filial affection of them all. Not only will they show affection to their own young, but they are ever ready to embrace and fondle any animal smaller than themselves, and that includes dead rats and mice.

At one time I was interested in breeding a good type of Alsatian dog, whilst, as usual, I kept a number of vervets as pets. One of my greatest worries was to prevent the pups from wandering over to where the apes were tied to trees. The moment a pup came within reach it would be seized and fondled; frequently they were held upside down whilst they were being subjected to this demonstration of affection. Any attempt to remove the pup generally resulted in its being carried up into the tree, where the cuddling and fondling would continue until the ape's attention was attracted by something else. The pup would then be abandoned up in the tree—often with serious consequences. I firmly believe that a vervet mother is fully capable of attacking a lion should it approach her baby too closely. That, in any case, happened to an enormous Great Dane dog who, in an affectionate gesture, started to lick a baby ape. The mother, who misinterpreted the dog's intentions, immediately flew at him and inflicted several serious gashes before he could escape from her fury.

CHAPTER XII

MOTHER 'MGANGA

" THE HYENA LAUGHS at his own stupidity, for when he picks up the bones other animals have left he thinks it is they who are stupid for leaving so much food behind and that makes him laugh. But what is it that makes you laugh like a hyena? "

This severe admonition was addressed to Ali, one of the best bush drivers I ever had. But that was about the only virtue he possessed, for Ali was a wayward, irresponsible native, possessed of a demoniacal temper, and frequently got himself into trouble for making fun of his elders—a serious breach of etiquette where natives are concerned.

The speaker on this occasion was " Mama 'Mganga " (mother witch-doctor), who for several weeks had frequented my native compound. Apart from her activities in matters pertaining to witchcraft, she also specialised in fortune-telling, and many were the wonderful predictions she had made to believers in my camp—predictions that never failed to materialise. The supernatural powers of Mama 'Mganga were extolled to me daily by the " knowing " members of my labour staff, and, for the want of something better to do, I had asked Black to arrange a sitting for me after he had told me of another of Mama 'Mganga's amazing prophecies which had come true only a few days earlier. Whatever claims Mama 'Mganga had to supernatural powers, she never entirely released her grip on mundane affairs, and her activities, to a large extent, centred around an important focal point—the coin of the realm. For a sum of five shillings she would peer deep into the future, or delve into the mysterious causes of misfortune, illness and death. The fact that she once sent one of my labourers on a thousand-miles journey to settle the score with a man who had caused the death of his wife by magic, goes to show what confidence her clients had in her diagnosis.

I am no believer in fortune-telling, nor in any of the mystic qualities so many people claim to possess, but five shillings is not an exorbitant sum to pay for an evening's entertainment, and although I had asked Black to arrange a seance for me, I was not at the time afflicted with any serious misfortune, nor was I suffering from any particular ailment that needed the help of a witch-doctor. The more immediate problem weighing on my shoulders, as indeed it does on those of many others, was to obtain a glimpse into the future. This was of considerable interest to me, for I had recently " struck it rich " when I located a small gold reef where values went as high as two ounces to the ton. A light ten-stamp battery which I had installed and got into operation was churning away and the results were satisfactory. But, like so many others who have tempted the gods in search of the elusive yellow metal, the question dominating my mind at the moment was: " How long will it last? " It was for this reason that I thought an appeal to Mama 'Mganga would not be out of place, for during the previous week my recovery of gold had reached as much as five ounces in a day, and if such a rate could be maintained steadily my dreams of wealth and luxury would not take very long to materialise. That week I had paid considerable tonnage bonuses to the labourers, the Saturday meat ration was trebled and a bag of Kaffir corn—an extra perk—was fermenting to provide the next week's beer supply. Everybody was happy, and the future looked rosier than it had for many, many months.

It was in this happy mood that I consulted Mama 'Mganga, paid my five shillings and sat down, fully expecting her to paint the future in even rosier hues. Mama 'Mganga's forecast, unfortunately, was not very encouraging. She told me that I would not remain in

my present surroundings for very long, and concluded:
" You are surrounded here by bush and dense forest;
I can see you in a vast open country where there are no
trees, no forest."

There was a lot more that had an ominous sound
about it, but I was not unduly upset by her discouraging
predictions—in spite of the fact that if they could be
relied upon, the indications were that the little reef would
not expand, nor would it go to any depth—a very common occurrence with small reefs giving high values near
the surface. Ali, however, was impressed with the good
fortune of the past week and could see no apparent
reason why we should vacate the property.

He came back with what he considered an appropriate
reply to Mama 'Mganga's severe rebuke. " The reason
why I laugh is that you have stolen five shillings from the
bwana and you are foolish enough to think that he will
believe your story. Any fool can see that we will be
here for years. The mine is rich, why should the bwana
leave it to go elsewhere? Perhaps you think he will run
away because he is afraid of the forests."

Mother 'Mganga was obviously angered by this insult
and the manner in which it was voiced. For a few
moments she glared at him with a malicious expression
in her eyes and then invited him to sit down next to her.

" So you laugh because I have stolen the bwana's
money and lied to him? " she began. " You are a very
clever young man indeed and you think you know better
than I do. But rest assured, my son, what I have told
your master is the truth; the only pity is that when the
time comes for him to leave this place you will not be
here, for you will be dead and buried." This forecast
was made with such hatred and malice that it savoured
of the passing of a death sentence.

Natives all have a healthy respect for witch-doctors
and all that pertains to the supernatural. Ali was no
exception to the rule, and he was visibly affected by
what he had heard, but his irresponsible, devil-may-care

nature soon asserted itself again and he left the fireside
chuckling and talking to himself.

Black, who had listened attentively to the proceedings
all evening, was deeply disturbed at the turn of events,
for he had implicit faith in the witch-doctor's ability to
foretell the future. " You should not have put a curse
on him, Mama," he said. " He is young and stupid and
meant no harm. It is good to frighten him, but he
should not die because he has offended you." There
was a good deal more talk about Ali and his indiscre-
tions, and when I left the fireside a few minutes later he
was still the subject of discussion.

The evening had certainly ended on a sombre note,
but I did not allow it to influence me unduly. Black,
on the contrary, was quite distressed and called on me
again before I turned in for the night.

" It will be well for you to find another driver for that
big truck of yours, Bwana. 'Mganga has been telling
me that Ali will die suddenly; he is reckless, and before
long he will have an accident and kill himself. Everything that woman has told me has come true; it is a pity
that she never tells one something that is cheerful."

He continued to give me several instances of the
accuracy of 'Mganga's prophecies. Impressive though
they were, I attributed it all to the law of retribution, for
although he was one of the most amiable characters I
ever met, Black was indeed a scoundrel of the first order,
and it did not need a fortune-teller to explain to him
that, sooner or later, some of his wild escapades would
come home to roost.

For the next fortnight the gold returns showed little
change and we had all forgotten about the witch-doctor's
predictions. Then, one Sunday morning, I arrived at
the plant to find several natives standing in a group,
holding a serious discussion. On inquiring, the headman told me that Ali had assaulted his wife during the
previous night and that she would probably die from her
injuries. I quickly went over to his hut and found the

I

woman suffering from ghastly head injuries—the result of an attack with a heavy stick.   Her condition appeared serious to me, and I immediately had her removed by car to the native hospital, twenty miles away.   Two days later I had occasion to visit the hospital on personal business, and the doctor informed me that the woman was recovering, but that she had had a very narrow escape.   Back at the mine that afternoon, I gave Ali a severe lecture and pointed out to him that he was lucky to escape a charge of murder.   I thought it was a good moment also to remind him of what the witch-doctor had said.   Ali was very repentant, and promised me that the offence would not be repeated.

For another three months all went reasonably well; the gold recovery was inconsistent: some days the returns were very good, then, for no apparent reason, there were days when they were very disappointing. We had now gone to considerable depth and were having frequent water and pumping troubles.   It was whilst I was underground late one Saturday night, attending to a faulty pump, that a native watchman came down to call me.   There had been serious trouble at a beer-drink, and Ali had once again assaulted his wife—more seriously than on the previous occasion.

" This time she will die," the watchman assured me. Once again I rushed over to find out just what had happened.   The woman was lying moaning and groaning on a rough camp-bed in a hut which was in complete darkness.   One glance at her in the rays of my torch convinced me that she was in a critical state.

The only car I had on the property was unfortunately out of order, but I immediately arranged for a Masheila and eight porters to carry her to hospital.   It was well past midnight when the porters started on their way. Ali was sitting outside his hut in one of his morose moods and seemed not the least bit interested in the proceedings.   He explained to me subsequently that the trouble was due to the fact that his wife had been too friendly with another native—a common occurrence when beer flows freely, as it did on this occasion. An argument had developed, during which he had knocked his wife down and then went to work on her with a pair of heavy miners' boots. I felt certain that the woman would not recover from her injuries, and had Ali locked up pending police action.

The next afternoon a European constable called on me to inform me that the woman had died; the assault had been a particularly brutal one and she had suffered serious damage to her liver and kidneys. Ali was removed to Mbeya, where he was held on a charge of murder. The case was tried a month later, and Ali was found guilty and sentenced to death.

After the trial, the chief Crown prosecutor, who had come from Dar-es-Salaam head office to conduct the case, informed me that the police were particularly anxious to secure a conviction on this occasion, as the year before Ali was tried for the murder of another woman and got off on account of the lack of conclusive evidence. This time they were determined that he should not escape, and it was for this reason that a senior official was sent to conduct the prosecution. Ali was hanged at the Tukuyu gaol six weeks later—in less than six months from the time Mother 'Mganga had foretold his death.

So far her prophecy about Ali had turned out correct. But what about the other part of it which pertained to me and the mine? By the time the case was being tried, the writing, as far as the mine was concerned, was already on the wall. It was war time, and the supply position became more and more difficult each day. As a result the gold output was reduced so seriously that the proposition became uneconomical. It was whilst I was in Mbeya for the trial that I accepted an offer for the property from a syndicate which was better equipped to face conditions. I sold out for a ridiculously low figure and the syndicate moved in.

During their second month of operations they struck it rich and the mine yielded over £5,000 profit—ten times the amount I received for it.   At that time I was hunting down in the Rift Valley in the vast open spaces where there are no trees and forest, just as Mama 'Mganga had predicted.   It was whilst I was there that the final story of the mine was written, for it was closed by the Mines Department after a serious accident in which a European and three natives were killed underground.   Thinking it all over now, had I remained on the property I might have been that European, for most of my time at the mine was spent underground.   I found consolation in the fact that, even though the wide open spaces did not offer the immediate means of amassing a fortune, they offered comparative safety—except for the occasional odd spot of bother with wild animals.

But to return to Mama 'Mganga.   On the night I called on her I certainly was no believer in fortune-telling.   I'm not at all sure that I believe in it now. But I cannot deny that she was remarkably correct in her predictions concerning Ali and myself.   My only regret is that I did not speculate another five shillings in order to peer a little deeper into the future!

CHAPTER XIII

A TROPHY WON—AND LOST

THERE IS NO other place where legends spring up so rapidly and hang on so tenaciously as they do in the African bush. In my time I have encountered the legendary elephant, lion, buffalo, gorilla, leopard, snake and, for good measure, the 'Mganga (witch-doctor). All of these can be extremely dangerous entities in native life, and it was therefore not surprising to come across them at widely separated points in various parts of the country and with but a slight variation in the matter of detail.

But when I came across the legendary eland bull, an animal which, for five years, so the story went, had defied every effort to lay him low, I began to wonder. The eland, the largest of all antelopes, is the most harmless and inoffensive of animals, and whereas trailing a lone bull in the bush is always a hopeless task because of the vast distances these solitary animals will cover in a day, hunting them in herds is not at all difficult, in fact, among the larger antelopes they are the easiest of all to hunt.

The story of this legendary bull, the largest ever seen in that part of Tanganyika, first came to my attention when as a newcomer I inquired about the prospects from the local hunting fraternity. Game, the natives assured me, was fairly plentiful, but the one animal that excited the imagination of every hunter in the district was this monster bull, who was always accompanied by seven or eight cows. Over the years they had all tried desperately to bag the bull and on several occasions they had managed to get him under fire, but no one had ever succeeded in doing any noticeable damage. Not only had the native hunters failed in all their efforts, but several European hunters who had come out to that part of the country to try to collect this outstanding trophy had fared no better than the native *fundis*—all of whom now believed that the bull was protected by a spirit which ensured its safety, and for that reason they had long since given up all hope of ever laying him low.

As I was due to settle in the district for a good many years in the mining business, I felt certain that, sooner or later, I would catch up with this outsize eland bull. According to the native hunters, the part of the country he and his entourage frequented most regularly was a small plain about ten miles long, six miles wide and not more than six miles from my camp. In this plain the grass never grew more than two feet high, and that was all in the bull's favour, for the slightest movement on the edge of the plain would send the herd off into the surrounding dense forest.

On a number of occasions when I went in search of the bull I found plenty of evidence to convince me of the presence of an extremely large specimen that was accompanied by a number of smaller animals. But as my hunting at the time was irregular, and dictated by necessity, I never gave much time or attention to this animal, and for my more important safaris I always preferred the Usanga plains, eighty miles away, where game was far more plentiful and large herds of buffalo could be found regularly. A day's hunting there would always ensure a better return than a week's hunting nearer home.

It was whilst talking one day to an old hunter in the township of Chunya, some thirty miles from my camp, that the subject of the big bull was mentioned to me for the first time by a European. He confirmed all of what the natives had told me previously, and I was surprised to hear that he had made at least a dozen trips especially to try to bag the bull—always without success. There were several other Europeans, he told me, who had made similar unsuccessful attempts to collect this outstanding trophy, but the best any of them had ever done was to admire his enormous size from a distance well beyond the range of any rifle. Apparently the bull had been under fire so often in the past that it was quite impossible to get within shooting range of him.

"The only way to collect that fellow," another European told me, "will be to walk on to him unexpectedly in the dense forest. Whilst he hugs the plain you will never get near enough to do any damage. He is a wily old bird and always makes sure to remain well within the herd—nothing very gentlemanly about him, for he is quite satisfied to let the cows protect him from any possible harm."

After listening to these accounts from more reliable sources, I made more frequent visits to the plain, and, like so many others, I was fortunate on a number of occasions to watch the herd through powerful binoculars. The bull was always in attendance, and there was no doubt at all about his size, but the problem was how to get him within shooting range. On a couple of occasions I had sent runners round the far end of the plain in the hope that they would drive the herd towards me at the near end, where I had taken up my position under close cover. But it was all to no good, and in the end I, like so many others, resigned myself to the belief that the big bull was not destined to die by human hand.

In the hope that some time or other luck might turn in my favour, I always carried a heavy ·404 rifle with me in addition to the light ·318 Accelerated Express which I used for smaller game on the open plain. But I finally gave up all hope of ever getting the bull under fire, and discarded the heavier rifle—a step I was to regret soon afterwards.

It was one morning at the beginning of March, after it had rained continuously for more than a week, that I decided to go out early and try to find something for the pot. Within half an hour of leaving camp I bagged a duiker, and in view of the threatening sky, I decided to return home. The natives, however, immediately set up a moan, and protested that a duiker, shared between two hundred labourers and five Europeans, would not be of much use to anyone. The plain, they pointed out, was only a few miles away, and in view of the fact that there had been no hunting for more than a fortnight, we could reasonably expect to find animals feeding there. In the end I gave in to them and agreed to carry on. The duiker was sent back home and we continued on our way.

We had not gone more than a mile when a heavy drizzle set in, and this continued for more than an hour. It was only because of a lot more moaning and pleading that I continued the walk towards the plain. Half an hour's walk brought us on the fresh tracks of a herd of roan antelope, and they, too, were heading for the plain.

The soft condition of the ground made tracking very easy and another mile or so brought us to the edge of the plain, where, some 200 yards from us, the herd was walking along in single file. I sat down, picked a fine big bull and squeezed the trigger of the ·318 Express. I could hear the bullet strike, and the spasmodic jerk as the bull took off convinced me that I had placed a heart-shot. The herd immediately made for the forest at the edge of the plain, with the wounded bull trailing behind. A few hundred yards farther on we found him in a cluster of dense bush.

The weather still looked threatening, and after the morning's soaking I was anxious to avoid standing in another downpour, and urged the natives to skin and dissect the animal quickly whilst I sat down to coffee and sandwiches. We were just about ready to allocate the meat-loads when one of the spotters jerked me by the shoulder and pointed out to the plain. There, some 700 yards from us, was the eland herd with the big bull in attendance, walking slowly in single file and making for the east side of the wooded country. The range was far too great for the light Express I carried, and I quickly rushed for a point several hundreds of yards ahead where the bush jutted deeply into the plain. Here I sat waiting for the herd to pass at a distance which I estimated would be roughly 300 yards. But before they reached that point, a fool native, following behind me in order to watch the shooting, put the animals on the alert, and the next instant they were running across the plain in a close group some 500 yards away.

Once again my hopes of collecting the prize bull were dashed to the ground; the only satisfaction I had was the knowledge that I had got closer to him than on any previous occasion and the closer view confirmed that he was indeed an outstanding specimen—both for size and horns. Black, my old gun-bearer, was soon in evidence.

"Our luck has changed at last," he declared. "Something tells me that bull has reached the end of the trail. It will be easy to track them down in this soft ground, and once they enter close forest we will catch up with them."

I was not very much impressed with Black's second sight, but his argument was perfectly sound; in the rain-sodden ground, and with two of my best trackers on the job, we should be able to hold the trail easily, and I had all day to devote to the job.

A few moments later we were on the trail. Tracking was very easy, and during the next three hours we succeeded in putting the herd up on two occasions, but, as ever, the bull was securely screened by the other members of the herd. It was an hour later when once again we spotted the herd on the run and well beyond shooting range. We had now been on the trail for more than four hours; the animals had entered dense mopani forest, and at best I could not hope to get a clear range of much more than 100 yards, and with the herd on the alert, I felt certain we would never be able to approach them so closely.

The whole affair appeared completely futile, and I decided to call it a day. The trackers were called off and we began walking back to our starting point of that morning, bemoaning our bad luck. But after little more than a mile the leading spotter brought us to a sudden stop. In the close mopani forest, roughly 200 yards away, two eland cows could be seen. They appeared to be keenly on the alert, but with the wind in our favour they were unaware of us and were more concerned about swishing flies from their backs. Of the bull, however, there was no sign.

" They are all clustered together in that bush," said the spotter in a whisper. " I saw the bull; he is a little deeper in the bush. If we remain here quietly they will start grazing soon, and the big fellow will break cover."

For the next half-hour we sat watching intently for the first movement that would bring the bull into sight. The animals had calmed down, but they were not moving. Then, suddenly, one of the trackers beckoned for me to crawl up to where he was sitting. From his point of observation a large dark-blue patch could be discerned. I knew from the colouring of the skin that it was the bull, but in that dense foliage it was quite impossible to tell whether it was part of his neck, side or stomach that was showing. It was certainly no target to take a chance on, and for the next five minutes we watched closely for a move, but that bull remained stationary. As we sat watching, the cow nearest to us looked in our direction in a startled manner—perhaps a breath of air had carried our scent to her; there was no more time to waste, and I decided to take the chance.

As the Express bullet hit the mark I could tell from the heavy thud that it had struck bone. In the next instant the entire herd came rushing towards us. There was, of course, no question of a charge, but the echo of the report from the forest beyond gave the impression that the shot had been fired from that direction. As the bull came out into the open, running on three legs, I placed another shot, and in little more than 100 yards he collapsed.

The moment he went down, the seven cows came to a sudden stop and started crowding around him, and in that position they remained until we had approached within fifty yards, and then they reluctantly trotted off. Several hours later, whilst waiting for more porters to carry the meat, we could still see them milling around restlessly in the nearby forest. With them the habit of protecting the old patriarch had developed into an instinct. Watching this pathetic demonstration of feminine devotion determined me never to shoot an eland again, and in this respect fate was kind, for I never found it necessary to do so.

The bull was without doubt the largest eland I had ever seen, and his dark-blue colouring showed that he was a very old animal. All that was in keeping with his legend; but a feature that no one had ever approached close enough to notice before, was the large and astonishing horn formation. Eland horns always grow out in a V spiral formation. The longer the horns, the wider the distance usually between the points—often as much as two feet will separate them. In this case the horns had reached their apex many years earlier and then turned inwards on a graceful curve and the two points had grown to within four inches of each other. It was indeed a magnificent and unique trophy, and I lost no time in sending the neck and horns to a firm of taxidermists in Nairobi for mounting.

So highly did they esteem the trophy that the day after it arrived in Nairobi they telegraphed asking me whether I was prepared to dispose of it and what my price would be. I had several letters from them subsequently on the subject, but I had decided to keep the mask for my own collection. Three months later I received their bill and the rail documents from Nairobi to Chunya via Tabora, and that, as it turned out, was the nearest I ever came to seeing my trophy again.   Somewhere en route it vanished from the face of the earth.

For a full year I kept up a regular correspondence with the railway authorities, and finally handed the matter over to the police for investigation.   All we could discover was that the case containing the head was handed over to a firm of Indian transporters at Tabora, some 300 miles from my camp, and from there the trail was lost.   It was many months later that an Indian Agent, supposedly acting on behalf of an Indian Rajah, and who I knew to be associated with the transport concern in question, came to me with a proposition.   His Highness, Mr. X of India, was anxious to procure for cash— or in exchange for good specimens of tiger mounts— some of the best specimens of African fauna.   As I had never heard of Mr. X before, and felt certain that he was unaware of my existence, I had a pretty good idea as to what happened to that exceptional trophy.   But India is a large place to start a hunt for a trophy that took over five years to collect.

CHAPTER XIV

LUCKY STRIKES

THE OLDEST AND deepest goldmine in Southern Rhodesia, and one which finally paid off over two million pounds, was bought for a case of candles. In spite of what one or two geologists and subsequent owners of the property have said to the contrary, this story is true; for on the day it happened I was living a few doors from the old trader who had sold a native two candles.

After paying for the candles, the native placed a piece of rich quartz on the counter of the trader and asked him if the stone interested him. It did, and in exchange for a case of candles the native showed him the place where he had found the quartz. The property was pegged, the mine worked for nearly fifty years and it was eventually closed on account of its great depth and water troubles. If anyone knows of an economic method of coping with these obstacles, the mine is still there, and he will have no trouble in securing the property and starting up afresh. When I passed the property only a few years ago a syndicate was busy working the ancient dumps and they were thinking of reopening the mine. I am not aware that they ever did.

In the early days in the Belgian Congo a prospector-hunter had the misfortune to damage the foresight of his rifle. A crude sight was remodelled out of candle-grease as two natives sat watching him. They had never seen a candle before, and when the prospector went out later in the day and shot two roan antelope in two shots, the natives believed that it was the " *muti* " which the man had put on his rifle that was responsible for his accurate shooting. They knew that he was looking for " green stones ", and the next day they brought him a bag full of these stones. They agreed to show him the place where they had found them in exchange for two pieces of " *mooti* ".

That was how the " Star of the Congo " mine was discovered. It happened quite fifty years ago, and the mine is still working today. The amount of copper it has produced during the years will exceed in value by far the sum of two million pounds.

When a European prospector sat outside his tent in the Belgian Congo one afternoon, a native brought him a piece of pitchblende rock and offered to show where it had come from in exchange for a small supply of tobacco. The prospector agreed, and he was taken to Chinkolobwe, the richest uranium mine in the world.

The story, which I firmly believe, relates that the prospector called on the Comite Special in Elisabethville, and in reply to his inquiries he was assured the area was open for pegging and outside the concession of the Union Miniere, the great copper-mining company of the Congo. It was after he had pegged the ground and applied for registration and it was discovered that the property was being pegged for *uranium*, and not for copper, that the authorities suddenly realised the ground was, after all, not open for pegging, and inside the Company's concession. The prospector received hearty thanks and a cheque for five hundred pounds, which he promptly tore up and threw into the donor's face before walking out in disgust. Within a couple of years of this discovery the Belgians dropped the price of radium by nearly half. This happened over thirty years ago, and Chinkolobwe still remains today the richest uranium mine in the world.

Two natives walked into a native beer-hall in Tanganyika one night and had their tongues loosened by an excessive intake of " *pombe* ". They told of a place where they had found several pieces of alluvial gold. These they agreed to trade in for beer. After the proceeds had been consumed, the owner of the beer-hall, a native woman, skilfully extracted the necessary information from them in exchange for a few more pots of beer. The information was passed on to a European digger whom she knew well. The digger's fortunes at the moment were at such a low ebb that he had to borrow ten shillings in order to pay registration fees for the claim.

Once on the property, he erected a rough digger's hut for himself and set a gang of natives to work. The hardest work the average digger in Tanganyika did in those days was to crawl out of bed late in the afternoon and weigh the day's takings. For a few days the digger in question stuck to his guns and weighed the meagre takings daily. Then, one day, he had his rest rudely disturbed by natives shouting and talking loudly as they came down the mountain footpath leading to his hut. Securely tied to two rough bush-poles hung an enormous rock which they deposited at the digger's door. The " rock " turned out to be a solid mass of gold, the largest of its kind ever found anywhere in the world, and weighed over eight hundred kilos, the value of which, after cleaning and purifying, would have amounted to something like fifty thousand pounds.

That " slug " was about the only worthwhile piece of gold ever found in that area. As usual, the news of the strike spread rapidly, and soon several hundred diggers were on the spot to try their luck, but not one of them found enough gold to pay his expenses. The gold-mining company for which I was working as secretary at the time added to my worries and troubles by taking the property over from the owner on a concession basis. A good many thousands of pounds were spent on sinking shafts and digging trenches, but never a pennyworth of gold did we find.

I have mentioned four outstanding cases here of rich discoveries that were made as the result of native information. It has never occurred to me to keep a detailed list of many scores of others, but I know of at least four large active mines operating today that were discovered in such circumstances, but they are of no particular importance to my story. The point I have tried to establish is that one can never afford to discard native information in such matters.

The other side of the story is that a great many natives have " got wise " to the white man's credulity and are forever ready to exploit his weakness in this respect, and whereas in the old days the odd candle or pound of tobacco proved useful mediums for negotiation, the modern trickster will talk only in terms of money. A particularly good-looking piece of quartz—usually stolen from a mine in production—is held up as a true sample of an ore body from which it is said to have been taken. Bargaining usually starts in the region of twenty-five pounds and generally comes down to five pounds. But payment is always demanded in advance. After that the victim is taken out to a barren outcrop and left to find gold that never existed.

Hunting and mining—in one capacity or another—have always been my main occupations in life, and over the years I have parted with several scores of fivers with a firm resolve that " this is the last time ". But even though I have never amassed a fortune as the result of native information, the fault on at least three occasions could be laid squarely on my own shoulders and was due to ignorance or lack of experience.

The first occasion was when a native brought me a piece of quartz heavily impregnated with gold. His price to show me the location of the ore-body was twenty-five pounds. After considerable bargaining it was decided that I would pay five pounds down in cash and if the property lived up to expectations another twenty-five pounds would be added to the initial deposit. The agreement concluded, the sample was handed in for assay, and I was astonished to find that it carried more than five ounces per ton. This happened in my early mining days and, like every other newcomer to the mining business, I began to visualise myself riding in a

Rolls-Royce and enjoying all the luxuries that form part of the life of a rich mine-owner.

The reef I was shown subsequently lived up to all expectations, the only disappointing feature was the small body and the steep angle at which it dipped. For three weeks we worked hard and followed the strike, the high values persisting. Then fate assailed me in the shape of a severe dose of malaria. The natives were left to follow the strike and dump the ore on the surface. It was quite ten days before I was able to return to work. By that time the gang had gone down another twenty feet, but now they were bringing up only barren rock.

" The reef has packed up," the headman informed me. " We have not seen a colour of gold for several days," he concluded.

It is just one of those things again, I decided, the same old story all over again, and I was happy when I succeeded in talking an old prospector into paying me three hundred pounds for the property and all the ore on the surface. But I had cause for self-abnegation a month later when the property was sold for twenty thousand pounds. What had happened in this case was that during my ten days' absence the natives had followed a barren leader that joined up with the reef and covered up the original body. This small body eventually led on to a large reef with high values.

The mine worked for several years before it finally closed down, and although the property was quite close to my home, I never again visited it, for I felt it was not necessary for me to have visual proof in order to remind me of my stupidity.

There was the other occasion whilst hunting on the borders of Northern Rhodesia and Tanganyika when a native came to me with a beautiful purply tinged stone, twice the size of my fist, and offered to show me the place where he had found it for a consideration of five pounds. My knowledge of precious and semi-precious stones was not such that I could identify the stone offhand, and

K

before coming to any final agreement it was decided that I should send the stone to a consulting geologist in Johannesburg. In due course the answer came back: it was a flawless amethyst. It only remained for me to find my man again—and the amethyst deposit. Finding the man was not difficult, but finding the deposit was quite another matter.

It transpired that the stone—and several others like it —was found by his father, who was the chief of that particular native settlement. This had happened some fifteen years earlier, and the old man had often spoken about it, but had never tried to cash in on his discovery. The reason was that he did not wish to attract Europeans to the area, believing as he did that trouble always followed in the trail of the white man. The old man had recently died, and the son had no doubt that, from the description of the place given by his father, he could easily find the deposit.

For the next six weeks we trailed through the most impossible, mountainous, soul-destroying country in Africa. Many a night I returned to camp too tired to eat or sleep. The only hopeful feature about it all was that " tomorrow is another day ". But in the end I decided that there were too many tomorrows and abandoned the search. That there is a deposit of great value somewhere in those mountains I have no doubt whatsoever, nor do I doubt that, sooner or later, someone on the trail of a wounded rabbit will walk on to it unexpectedly.

If accounts which I have no reason whatever to disbelieve are reliable, the richest gold deposit in Northern Rhodesia lies somewhere near Fort Jameson. Here an old prospector has gone down nearly 100 feet on a small reef of fabulous wealth and made a daily recovery of over three ounces by using pestles and mortars. At the end of his first year's operations the old man decided to return to England for a while. With a sound knowledge of native psychology, he had called in the chief of the district and the local witch-doctor and several hundreds of the inhabitants and there laid a curse on anyone who would betray his secret. After that he had buried the few tools he used in his operations and had the shaft covered over with leaves and branches before his departure.

That happened twenty years ago. The old prospector never returned, nor has anyone ever heard from him since. After his departure, one bold member of the community had dared the spirits and brought a European to the spot. The pair had descended the vertical shaft, and at the bottom they were welcomed by a black snake which might have been a mamba or a cobra. They both died shortly after they got back to surface.

There are thousands of civilised, educated people all over the world who believe that the members of the expedition who died after opening Tutankhamen's grave were victims of a curse. In the part of Northern Rhodesia where this fabulous reef is located every single member of the native population believes that a quick way to sudden death is to betray the secret of its where-abouts. I tried for more than a year to persuade them to give me even a rough indication of its location, but not one would listen. The nearest I got to it was when I recruited the help of an old half-caste who was born in that part of the country. When I saw him last he told me he was " making headway slowly ". His progress, however, was too slow for me, and I left the country still wondering just where that reef was situated.

My last but one adventure in search of fortune buried in the bowels of the earth was when I sent a prospector to a Central African territory in search of a rare and extremely valuable mineral. After a costly search which lasted for more than six months, he " struck it rich " one day and located a deposit of many thousands of tons of ore. When he returned with several bags of samples and we compared them with the specimens of the desired mineral, they appeared absolutely identical; a rough fire test also gave the right results. It certainly was an occasion for celebrating, and celebrate we did.

Once again we were counting the proceeds in millions, but when the assay report came through, it showed that the most valuable quality of our ore was its appearance, for it contained none of the metal we were looking for and had no commercial value at the time.

It was just over two years later that a consulting engineer from Johannesburg called on me to inquire about the worthless deposit we had found. In the meantime it had been discovered that the mineral contained a metal that was in great demand for modern aeroplane construction and quite as valuable as the one we sought in the first place. At last, I thought, the goddess of fortune had relented, for there were thousands of tons of ore in view on the surface, underground there would be many more thousands of tons. But there was still one more difficulty to contend with before securing all this wealth, and that was to register the property. When I called on the Registrar of Titles in order to complete this small formality, I was informed that the entire area had been closed to prospection only a few months earlier and would remain closed for at least ten years. In these ten years anything may happen, but if all goes well, I hope to be on the spot—just in case!

CHAPTER XV

AROUND THE CAMP-FIRE

THE HUNTING GAME provides many " highlights ", and if you were to ask ten professional hunters what they consider the most satisfying feature, you would probably be given ten different answers. Who can blame the hunter who will vote for the moment when he brought down a prize trophy in the shape of an elephant bull with a pair of outsize tusks, perhaps after a trail that had lasted several days? Or the man who had been scouring the countryside for days searching for a man-eating lion and had brought the trail to an end with a well-placed shot? Or the man who had had a spot of bother with a wounded buffalo bull and had stopped the charge with only a couple of yards to spare?

Yes, these are undoubtedly among the highlights of the game, for they bring excitement and thrills and, when it is all over, a large measure of satisfaction. I have experienced all these emotions in a variety of settings. But there is one feature, one emotion in the hunting game, that never failed to make a strong appeal to me and always made me feel that the game was worth the candle, and that was the evenings around the camp-fire after a day's successful hunt.

The pot has been empty for days, for you have struck barren country, or bad luck. The hunting gang is sulky and listless—too tired to walk another yard. With them the meat supply is an infallible barometer of their ever-changing moods. Then, when depression has reached the lowest ebb, the luck changes suddenly towards the end of another day of tiring tracking. You have struck it rich and dropped one or two large antelopes or an outsize buffalo bull. In a second fatigue and listlessness have vanished and there is feverish activity all round, for tonight the flesh-pots will be full. Tonight they will sing and dance and re-live the events of the day.   If there is a good brew of " *pombi* " in camp all gloom is dispelled and there will be a hilarious celebration.

It was such an occasion that last day in camp before we were due to move off to the Rift Valley for a three months hunt, after which we would be absorbed in the yearly campaign against the red locust.   The last time fortune had smiled upon us was ten days earlier, when I had bagged a buffalo bull.   The meat of that animal was consumed in a matter of five days, and now, for five long days, the trail had provided us with nothing but sweat and blistered feet.

That morning, before setting out on the trail again, Black, my old gun-bearer, and the most amiable of rascals, had come to me to borrow ten shillings.   This was the amount of money he needed to procure an ample supply of beer from a nearby village for our last night in camp.   The occasion was the parting—perhaps for ever —between Black and his two wives.   I had made it clear that no women would be allowed to accompany our safari, in view of the fact that later we would join up with some two thousand five hundred native members of the red locust staff.   With a preponderance of over five hundred males to every female, women can be, and always are, the source of endless trouble and quarrels.

The ten shillings Black had borrowed from me that morning would ensure a liberal supply of beer for the gang, but it would not contribute in any way towards securing the necessary meat supply that would help to make Black's farewell party a memorable affair.   The only way to procure the necessary meat would be to hunt for it and hope for better luck than we had had for so many days.

For a great many years my hunting staff had consisted mainly of natives of the Mwemba tribe.   They are excellent all-round hunters, tireless on the trail, masters of bushcraft and come second only to the pygmies of the Congo in the art of tracking and spotting.   In addition, they are passionately fond of music, have a great sense of humour and are, without doubt, the finest mimics I ever came across. With them the day's hunt never finishes in the field, but is brought right back into camp. The smallest event of note during a hunt is re-enacted around the camp-fire at night with great detail. If during the day you have missed an easy shot, lost the trail—or your temper, escaped a charge by the skin of your teeth, got a shock when a buck jumped out from under your feet in long grass, the scene will be humorously portrayed around the camp-fire that night. Always the evening will come to a close with the singing of popular melodies, beautifully harmonised.

The only member of my staff on this occasion who did not belong to the Mwemba tribe was Black, who was a Nyasa, and for that reason, the pet subject of the Mwembas' humorous puns. Unlike other natives, Black never took the trail without a pair of outsize hobnail boots on his feet—many sizes too big for him.

This morning we were on the way early to make a last determined effort to replenish the meat supply before leaving the next day. The fun started early, when we arrived at the edge of a large open clearing. Some 200 yards away an old warthog was trotting slowly across the clearing. He suddenly became aware of our presence, and with head and ears erect, he stood glaring in our direction. A second later I squeezed the trigger of my light sporting rifle and the warthog collapsed in a heap. In spite of the heavy boots, Black was soon many yards in the lead to secure the prize. When only a few yards separated him from the kill the warthog suddenly revived. My shot was a little too high and merely creased the brain, and now, in a towering rage, the big pig came straight for Black. The charge had got under way so quickly and Black was running so fast towards the animal that he was unable to change direction in time to get out of the way, but, with great presence of mind, he managed to leap clear over the back of the charging pig. A second later

Black was screaming loudly for help with the pig close on his heels.   For some reason which I have never been able to determine, he started to run in circles whilst the warthog gradually reduced the distance between them.

At this stage of the proceedings, the Mwembas, who stood watching from a safe distance, were splitting their sides with laughter, not realising that they were obstructing my line of fire.   It was quite thirty seconds later that I was finally able to line the pig up in my sights; by that time Black was screaming louder than ever and stepping it out at a speed seldom attained by man.   When it was all over he slumped to the ground, where he sat spluttering as he gave voluble thanks to all the gods that be for his timely deliverance.

" *Aki* [truthfully], Bwana, that is the nearest I have been to death for many a long day.   If that ugly brute was not so badly stunned he would have picked me up long before you could come to the rescue.   Tonight I will eat his liver and stomach for all the trouble he has caused me," he said.

Black's assessment of the danger that had threatened him was by no means exaggerated.   Besides being the ugliest animal on earth, the warthog is also an extremely dangerous beast when roused.   With his sharp, powerful tusks he is capable of inflicting terrible injuries, and there are many cases on record where a warthog, fighting for its life, has proved more than a match for a male lion.

If the day started on a comical note—from the spectators' point of view—it ended happily for us all, for a few hours later I managed to bag two large antelopes.   That night the beer flowed freely around the camp-fire, the flesh-pots were full and Black was there in the role of host, smiling benignly upon his guests.   But that was before the Mwembas got busy.   During the afternoon they had cut enormous slabs of rubber from an old cartyre.   These they had tied to their feet, and now they were busy giving a true-to-life illustration of the events of the morning.   The exhibition finally became so embarrassing to Black that he threatened to shut off the beer-taps and call a halt to the entertainment.

" If I looked one half as bad as these Mwembas would have one believe, it would have been better if that ugly pig had killed me," he remarked to me.

Black's farewell party lasted for most of the night, and early the next morning the truck was loaded and we were on our way to the Rift Valley camp—fifty miles away. Some ten miles farther on we stopped at a small native village for a short while, and later that afternoon we reached our destination.

The camp was hurriedly prepared, and shortly after dark the camp-fire was burning brightly, the entire gang having taken up their positions near the fire. Black only was sitting some distance away in the shadows. Thinking that he was anxious to avoid seeing a repetition of the previous night's demonstration, I walked over to him—to find him in earnest conversation with the two wives for whom he had given the farewell party the previous night. They had mounted the truck at the small village where we had stopped earlier in the day. I could not very well order the women to return home at that time of night, so I did the next best thing, and that was to give Black a sound beating.

Months later he had more serious cause for regret, when one of the native members of the locust staff stuck a knife into him during a quarrel over one of his wives. It was a fortnight later before he was able to move about again, but by that time the two faithless wenches had " married " two other members of the staff.

" They cost me one pound each," he complained to me, " and that money I will never recover."

My equipage on safari on occasions was a strange one indeed. My late wife, Doris, a famous concert pianist, gave up concert work in order to take to the life in the bush. If she abandoned the concert platform, it did not mean that she lost interest in the piano, and without it I do not think she would have remained in the bush for very long. The difficulty was overcome by having a good full-size piano in our home, whilst on long safaris we usually carried a little miniature instrument which gave excellent results and could be handled almost as easily as a large provision box.

During the months of August and September, the weather in most parts of Central Africa is ideal for hunting safaris. This is the dry season, and at this time of the year the grass has been burnt down, and water can usually be found only in isolated pools. It is in these areas near the pools where game is most plentiful. Apart from the gemsbok and the eland, all African fauna like to drink at least once a day.

The camp we occupied on this occasion had been prepared with considerable care for a lengthy sojourn, and we were now in the second week of hunting. Large piles of meat, dried and smoked, were stacked up for eventual dispatch to the main depot at the mine. The beer-brews were fermenting regularly and the flesh-pots were full. The camp-fire at nights presented a scene of gaiety, for there the events of the day would be discussed at length and any worthwhile event that happened in the field during the day would be re-enacted in full detail.

Around the fire the blacks would sit with lumps of meat on long spits, gorging themselves with meat and beer. Excessive drinking was never tolerated, and by 9 p.m. the camp would usually be ready for our entertainment. The Mwembas would sing their songs of the hunt, of the wives and homes they had left behind. Ndege, the master tracker, would dance with a spear in hand and a leopard skin around his loins and demonstrate how he sat near a water-hole one night, muzzle-loader in his hand, and waited for a buffalo herd to come to drink, and how he killed the leader of the herd with one shot in the dark. Clarrick, the other super tracker, who could tell almost to a minute, by looking at a broken leaf, how much time had elapsed since the herd passed that spot; Hoppes, the amazing spotter whose eyes could match those of a vulture—these two would sing and dance and demonstrate how, in their time, they had tracked down the wiliest of game. There was a special number in which they demonstrated that day when they had tracked a marauding lioness to her den, killed her with spears and captured her two young cubs.

These two, Clarrick and Hoppes, were blood brothers, which meant that they were from the same mother (" brothers " otherwise signifies that they are from the same village or tribe). These two blood brothers had obviously lived through many hair-raising adventures together. Also, they had had plenty of time to compose some of the most impossible hunting stories ever invented by man. When they had all said their piece, Doris would turn to the piano and play hymns and old plantation songs. The blacks would join in and sing and harmonise until it was time for bed.

On such occasions one is carried far away into an imaginary world and all that is real is the surrounding forest and the camp-fire. Soon the blacks would start to straggle off, one at a time, until the camp-fire was deserted. Doris and I would sit and talk a while, and again there would be the strains of beautiful music, a Chopin nocturne or some other soul-stirring melody, and then we also would turn in for the night.

It was on nights such as these that the hunt brought me far more happiness and contentment than the killing of any prize trophy. It was on such a night, brightly moonlit, that the proceedings around the camp-fire were interrupted by the sudden appearance of a stranger—a man in his late twenties, bearded, unkempt and fatigued. Following immediately behind him were two native porters who carried his kitbags and blankets and the few rough implements he required on his journey. We looked up in surprise at this stranger, whose unexpected arrival at the camp-fire puzzled us greatly. He stood looking around for a moment, until his eyes alighted upon me, and then walked over to where I was sitting on a log.

" Pardon me, signor," he said as he offered his hand. " Are you the hunter the natives speak of as Bwana Congo? "

I answered that that was what I was called and then suggested that the stranger rested and took some refreshment.

" Thank you," he said. " But first let me introduce myself. My name is Pedro Montagno. Your offer of food is very welcome, for I am extremely fatigued after today's long trek. You no doubt have curiosity as to my presence here—that I shall satisfy as soon as I have rested."

The immediate needs of the strange and unexpected visitor were attended to promptly. In snatches of conversation he told of the week he had spent wandering through the bush—not aimlessly, but to an unspecified point where he would eventually find means of transport to take him to the Belgian Congo. The conditions there, and the fact that he spoke French fluently would, he thought, help his future movements.

As I had spent many years in the Congo previously, we sat talking about conditions in that country for a long time. After that the conversation drifted to current affairs. Pedro, it appeared, had not been in Africa very long, and somewhere along the road his plans had come unstuck. He was keenly interested in hunting and asked many questions. Seeing a piano in the bush intrigued him, and Doris, in response to his request, played for him. His choice of music was extraordinarily good. But Signor Pedro was obviously tired, and a little later we prepared to turn in for the night.

" My story may not appeal to your good lady; shall we leave it until the morning? " he said as he prepared to leave for a rough shack I had placed at his disposal.

I agreed that the next day would be as good as any, and with that we bade each other goodnight. If anything, we were more puzzled than we were at the moment of his arrival.

Shortly after daybreak the next morning I was out on the trail. The hunting was good, and by 11 a.m. I was back in camp. Lunch, as usual, was a hurried affair, and by 3 p.m. the meat was all properly dissected and placed on smoking ramps. Pedro had watched proceedings with great interest. Now, with the butchery side of the business attended to, I instructed the gun-bearer to take all my rifles to a big tree, in the shade of which I usually attended to the daily cleaning and checking. A few minutes later we were seated on a log in the shade.

" You are no doubt anxious to hear my story? " he commenced.

" Well, the circumstances of your arrival in camp last night are rather unusual. I am naturally curious to know what it is all about," I replied.

" As you will probably have guessed, I am in trouble with the law. I was on a tour of Africa when I met a girl in Lourenço Marques. It is the same old story all over again, only I did not know she was under age. Her father is one of the most important men in Mozambique; the trouble was fast coming to a head when a friend of mine in the police warned me that he was applying for a warrant for my arrest and advised me to get out as quickly as possible and make my way back to Europe via the Congo. In my position such a scandal would mean complete ruin for me, and my parents will certainly disown me. I took the advice of my friend and left Lourenço Marques by goods-train. I am not accustomed to travelling in the bush, and what I have seen of it so far convinces me that I will never reach the Congo alive. What would you advise me to do?"

So that was the story! Pedro had travelled more than 1,000 miles during the three weeks he had been on the run, but most of that distance had been done on trains and by lifts from passing motorists. The 200 miles or more through the bush before such help would again be available to him would be a suicidal attempt in his case, for he was unarmed and completely ignorant of the obvious dangers of such an undertaking. I strongly advised him to abandon all thought of a trek across country, for, apart from all other considerations, the bush is the last place to seek safety from the law, as natives will immediately report any European travelling through the country in suspicious circumstances. I urged him to think matters over carefully and remain in camp until we could decide on something more practical. The fact that he had come so far without interference, I pointed out, seemed to indicate that he was not on the " wanted " list. After our conversation he returned to his shack, deep in thought.

That night the camp-fire was burning early, and soon the nightly concert was in full swing. As the natives finished a particularly lively song and dance, Pedro turned to Doris.

" Would you play something for us, madam? A Neapolitan song or some other popular melody? If you have no objection I will accompany you, but I warn you, my voice will never bring me fame."

Pedro sang two songs in a very pleasing voice, and then asked to be excused as he walked off to his shack. A few moments later he was back with a mandoline in his one hand and a folder of pamphlets in the other. The first pamphlet he handed me read: " Sgr. PEDRO MONTAGNO, Europe's Leading Mandolinist, at the Theatre Olympia, Paris, at 9 o'clock tonight." There were several others proclaiming him as the leading exponent of the mando-line.

That, then, was the set-up that night, with two celebrities performing around a camp-fire, deep in the forest. That night the Mwembas were pushed into the background and we sat listening to a concert that would have graced any music-hall. After that the camp-fire concerts became a nightly feature. In the meanwhile I had sent off a runner to the nearest District Commissioner to make discreet inquiries. Ten days later the runner came back with the reply: " There will be no objections to Signor Montagno passing through the country so long as he reports at the different administrative posts en route."

A week later Pedro was on his way to South Africa, and it was quite two months later when we heard from him again. Enclosed in a long letter describing his journey south was a pamphlet announcing that he was appearing at the Tivoli Theatre in Cape Town. When next we heard from him he was back in Europe, and for a long time we received autographed records from him. He was then recording for His Master's Voice. It is many, many years ago since last I heard from Signor Pedro; perhaps he is no longer living. He was undoubtedly a very fine artist, and I doubt whether he ever played better than he did on those nights around our camp-fire. For obvious reasons I have given him a fictitious name.

Another strange and delightful character who on occasions helped to cheer our camp-fire nights was a brilliant brain specialist. When I first met Dr. Bernard on official Company business he assumed an air of importance that some people found difficult to tolerate. In fact I found it awkward to deal with him, and hoped I would never have to have too much to do with him.

Some months later he arrived at my main camp after he had been out in the broiling sun all day with car trouble. I was fortunately able to help him, but whilst we stood talking on the veranda, Doris, in one of her inspired moods, was giving a rare performance on the Ibach Grand.

" You have an excellent radio here," the doctor commented as she was working up to a crescendo.

" Oh, yes, Doctor," I replied; " that is a Doris High Fidelity—the best in Africa."

" I have never heard of it before," replied the doctor.

" In that case you had better step inside and get acquainted."

As we entered the room Doris came forward to meet us. " Let me present you to the set you have just heard in action," I said as I introduced them.

The doctor was completely nonplussed, as, apart from the piano, there was no other musical instrument in the room. The joke was explained to Doris, and she readily agreed to play for him.

It was quite two hours later when the doctor left the room without a trace of his haughtiness. Following this episode, he became a regular visitor to our camp, and sooned joined in our week-end hunting trips. On these occasions we always carried the little piano with us, for the doctor was passionately fond of music and quite an accomplished musician himself.

Whilst sitting around the camp-fire one night, there was a disturbance at the meat-pile and the natives reported lion. We immediately set out with a torch in search of the raider, the doctor trailing close on my heels. We had walked little more than 200 yards when there was a loud grunt right next to me as I all but walked on to a hyena which for a moment I took to be a lion. I was concentrating so deeply on the cause of the disturbance that I forgot all about the doctor. After ascertaining the cause of the alarm I turned round, expecting him to be close on my heels, but there was no sign of him anywhere.

It was after I had called loudly several times that I heard him shouting back from the camp-fire, where I found him a few minutes later in a most unenviable state. In his headlong rush for camp in the dark, the doctor had run into a " wait-a-bit " thorn-bush. His legs were badly scratched and there was practically nothing left of his trousers. In his semi-nude condition he presented an extremely comical sight, but by this time he had long since dropped his haughty, superior manner. A few moments later he was stepping it out for all he was worth in company with the Mwembas, who were doing a high-stepping war-dance for our special benefit.

The idea of joining the natives, whose clothes, for the greater part, were as torn and tattered as his own, made a great appeal to his sense of humour. It was fortunate that I had brought along a spare pair of trousers, which, although nearly twice his size, prevented him from returning to headquarters in little more than his birthday suit.

There was yet another night when we sat around the camp-fire until late. After the blacks had gone to bed, my friend Charlie Goss, the elephant-hunter, and I prepared to turn in. Our camp was in a large open clearing on the bank of a small creek. On the opposite side of the creek were some trees, on the branches of which we hung the proceeds of the day's hunting. We were just dozing off when a native came to tell us that a hyena was trying to raid the meat.

I was not very disturbed, as I thought the meat was well out of reach of any hyena, and even if the prowler did help himself to a piece, the damage would not amount to much. Charlie, however, was not satisfied and sat in bed with his torch playing on the meat. Nearly an hour later I was awakened from a deep sleep when he fired a shot.

" That hyena will give us no more trouble," he remarked as he turned in.

We were lying waiting for coffee early the next morning when the blacks started a great commotion on the opposite bank of the creek. We inquired from the cook what it was all about.

He calmly replied, " They are excited about that lion you shot last night."

A lion it was indeed—just another of his tribe who was

L

suffering from the after-effects of an encounter with a porcupine. He had several broken quills sticking in his paws and was thoroughly emaciated. He had probably not eaten for several days when he tried to raid the meat.

The great Selous, with whom I once spent several weeks on a safari in the Shangani district of Southern Rhodesia, was one of the strangest characters I ever saw around the camp-fire.

Selous usually set out early in the morning in the quaintest of garbs, which consisted of a helmet, a khaki shirt and a pair of *veld-schoens*. Dressed in this manner, he would spend the whole day on the trail, or around camp, but at sunset he would withdraw to his tent, bathe and emerge immaculately attired in a dress suit. At the camp-fire he would join us and talk for hours about his adventures and the habits of game animals, which he knew better than anyone else.

Yes, it is true the camp-fire does not provide the thrills of the hunt, nor the excitement, but it has an appeal of its own and is the culminating point of a successful day in the field.

CHAPTER XVI

THE LEOPARD UNTAMED

I F Y O U W E R E to ask ten habituees of the African bush their choice for the most beautiful animal in the forest, the chances are that eight will vote for the leopard. Ask the same ten which they consider the most detested and destructive beast, and all ten will most likely vote for the same animal. Of all the beasts of prey, there is no other animal that kills so indiscriminately for the lust of killing alone like the leopard.

Gaining entrance to an enclosure where sheep, goats or fowls are kept, he will kill as many as time permits, and if he is left unchecked, he will leave the enclosure a bloody shambles without a single survivor. After this blood-bath, he will select a few tit-bits to appease his hunger. The remainder is left to testify to the animal's insatiable lust for killing.

The same ten people will also say that the best treatment you can give such a ferocious and treacherous beast is to line him up in the sights of a powerful rifle and squeeze the trigger—making sure that your first shot is an outright killer, for no animal in the bush is quicker to resent injury and repay evil with evil than the leopard. Mortally wounded, his last dying effort will be to level the score, cost what it may. In this respect he is far more determined and impetuous than the lion, who, as often as not, will seek safety in flight when the going gets too tough. When the occasion arises, the subject of an attack will frequently fare better facing an outraged lion than the smaller, but more agile and more cunning leopard.

I do not wholly agree with these opinions. To my mind there is no more beautiful animal to be found anywhere than a prize specimen of leopard. His blood-thirsty and savage instincts, I admit, are black spots against his character.   But to suggest that because of his evil and destructive habits he is devoid of any redeeming feature is completely wrong.   I should know, for over a span of twenty years or more I have successfully raised five leopards, four of which attained full maturity, and the first of this quintette was my inseparable companion for seven long years until he was killed by a " sportsman " hunter who also had the killing lust developed to a very high degree.

I was sitting outside my tent in the Belgian Congo one morning when a number of porters carrying a rough bush-made *mashila* came running into camp.   On the stretcher lay a badly mauled native, and behind the porters came yet another native carrying a small leopard cub.   The wounded man was the victim of the cub's mother, who had attacked him immediately he approached her den.   But for the fact that the man's companions were armed with spears and pangas, there would have been no need for them to carry him to camp for such medical treatment as I could give him.

The leopard was dispatched after she had inflicted a number of ghastly wounds on her victim.   I attended to the wounds as best I could before sending the injured man off to the nearest hospital, where he died shortly afterwards.   After considerable bargaining I finally persuaded the others to part with the cub for a sum of twenty-five francs, which at that time amounted to about two shillings and sixpence.   My twenty years' association with the leopard family had begun!

" Spots ", as a cub, presented no difficulties to raise. He soon took to playing with the dogs, cats and vervets which I kept as pets.   At this stage of his development he was daily subjected to a rough handling by the other pets, and a big baboon which I often let loose to join in the fun took a great delight in making life as miserable for " Spots " as possible.   The friendship of the two ended on a bad note some two years later when " Spots " was almost full-grown and " Boon ", the ape, once again resorted to rough tactics. A few seconds later they were at each other's throats.

The struggle was so fierce and the two were so closely interlocked that I was powerless to interfere. After a savage fight which lasted fully ten minutes, " Spots " emerged the victor. But he did not escape unmarked, for the baboon had torn him badly with his long fangs. For "Boon" the fight ended tragically, for he lay dead with a severed jugular vein. For quite half an hour " Spots " would not allow me to approach him—or his victim; at the end of that time he had almost completely devoured the hind leg of his old friend!

But as a pet, " Spots " never showed any aggressive tendencies towards me, and in the end he became the most reliable " watch-dog " I ever had. Elsewhere I have related how he finally accounted for a persistent burglar who for months defied all police efforts to capture him. By this time there was such a perfect understanding between us that I often allowed him to take pieces of meat from my mouth, and frequently, when he was hungry and busy chewing a piece of meat, he would raise no objection if I took it away from him; the most he would do would be to give a terrific display of snarling and spitting, and in the end yield the swag gracefully.

Some months before I was due to leave the Congo, the eventual disposal of " Spots " presented me with considerable concern. It was just at that time that H.R.H. the Duke of Kent was due to visit the Congo. An organising committee thought it would be a good idea to present the Duke with a fully domesticated leopard, and two members of the committee travelled 100 miles to Jadotville, where I lived, to collect " Spots ".

In his cage " Spots " had no objection to being petted and stroked by the strangers whilst I was present, and later that afternoon he was put in a cage and the party left for Elisabethville. The next day there was a frantic telephone appeal for me to proceed to Elisabethville immediately, as " Spots " had been allowed to escape from his cage, which fortunately had been placed in a storeroom. He would not permit anyone to approach him and had clawed the caretaker who tried to subdue him. When I arrived on the scene I found him running around the room in a towering rage, spitting and snarling at the onlookers. As soon as he spotted me he calmed down immediately, and a few moments later he sat purring in my arms and licking my face.

After this experience I decided it would be better for me to take him along to Tanganyika, where I had decided to settle down to the hunting business again. Here " Spots " was frequently allowed to accompany me on my outings in search of game, and at first his keenness and alertness raised my hopes of training him to capture small game. But in this respect he turned out a complete failure, for, unlike the cheetah, who will run down his prey, the leopard's instinct is to approach by stealth and spring upon an unsuspecting victim. But here his lack of natural training in his youth proved a serious handicap, and all his efforts were doomed to failure.

Early one morning, accompanied by a friend, I went out in search of game. " Spots ", as usual, was trailing behind us. At one stage my friend and I became separated, each following a different trail. A few moments later a shot rang out to my left some 200 yards away. Almost immediately afterwards my friend was shouting at me at the top of his voice, but owing to the distance separating us I was unable to hear what he was saying. Thinking that he could be needing my help, I walked quickly in the direction from whence the shouts came. " Spots ", with hair raised over his neck and shoulders, was running ahead of me in the same direction.

Suddenly there was a vicious snarling and spitting ahead of me, and when I looked in the direction of the disturbance I was horrified to see two leopards engaged in a life-and-death struggle, barely twenty yards away. It was obviously too dangerous for me to try to separate the struggling animals, and they were locked so closely together that it was impossible for me to get a clear shot at the intruder. Once again I was forced to stand and watch a battle to death which lasted fully a quarter of an hour before " Spots " got the upper hand over his wounded adversary and fastened his fangs in its throat; a few seconds later it was all over. But " Spots " emerged from this struggle in such bad shape that we had to have him carried home. It was quite two months before the wounds were completely healed.

I have often shuddered to think what would have happened to me that day if, without the intervention of " Spots ", I should have walked on to a badly wounded leopard!

Incidents such as I have described here, the excellent services " Spots " rendered me as a " watch-dog ", and my close association with leopard pets for a period of over twenty years, during which time I never had the slightest trouble with any of them, convinced me that, with proper care and a firm control, the big spotted cats can become useful and lovable creatures. It was for this reason that I rarely went out gunning for one of them. But there came the day when a member of the leopard family taxed my patience and forbearance to such an extent that I finally decided to settle the score.

I was in my hunting camp away down in the Back Congo at the time. A week or so after we reached this camp, sleep at night became quite impossible owing to the persistent barking of dogs and the snarling of a prowling leopard. A few nights later one of my prize dogs fell victim to the big cat. Two nights later the performance was repeated and I lost another valuable hunting dog.

My patience was beginning to run low, but I decided that rather than resort to reprisals, I would lock the two remaining dogs in an enclosure where they would be safe from the leopard. It was only then that I realised that the nightly trouble had been due mainly to the fact that the leopard was after some fowls which I kept in a nearby enclosure where the proceeds of the day's hunting were piled up for the night. Without disturbance from the dogs, the leopard promptly devoted his attention to the enclosure, and one night, when there was a terrific commotion among the fowls, one of my natives, believing the intruder to be a wild cat or a civet, rushed up with a heavy club in hand in order to dispatch the prowler. It was as he entered the forced gate and blocked the doorway that the leopard made his dash for safety. The native was knocked to the ground and subjected to a terrific mauling—one of his ears being completely torn away.

This was the last straw, and early the following morning, accompanied by the two remaining dogs and a gang of natives, we set out on the trail of the culprit. I carried a double-barrel 12-bore shotgun, loaded with S.S.G. ammunition (to my mind the finest weapon against soft-skin animals in close bush), whilst my two trackers were armed with medium rifles. The dogs were quickly on the trail, and in less than an hour the leopard was driven up a high tree with enormous outstretched branches. From there he sat snarling and spitting at us.

I instructed the trackers to hold their fire whilst I attended to him with my shotgun. But it was not quite as easy as I had anticipated, for a large branch behind which the leopard sat snarling at me obstructed the target, and I immediately started circling around so as to get a clear line of fire. At last I had him well in my sights, but it was the merest fraction of a split second before I squeezed both triggers that he made his leap for me. I was almost directly beneath him. But with the full force of two barrels, fired at almost point-blank range, there was no doubt at all as to the outcome, but that flying mass came at me at such a speed that it was impossible for me to get out of the way in time.

I was knocked to the ground, and when I regained my senses it was to find myself suffering from a badly dislocated shoulder and several other injuries. As for the leopard, he lay dead beside me with his head hanging on to a small piece of skin which the double load had failed to sever.

"What a fool to stand beneath a treed leopard!" I can imagine readers saying. I quite agree, but I have yet to meet the active hunter in the African bush who did not, at some time or another, do foolish things. In the course of time this kind of recklessness and carelessness seems to grow on one, and that explains why so many experienced hunters are killed by dangerous animals. In my own case I can clearly remember at least a dozen occasions when luck alone saved me from getting my deserts.

After this incident I had only one more worthwhile adventure with one of the spotted cats, but I gradually built up an enormous collection of over one hundred fine skins, which I bought or traded in for meat, from native hunters and villages where leopards were poisoned or killed in traps. These skins I cured and softened thoroughly, and in one or two cases I was paid as much as fifteen pounds for a prize trophy.

It was this indiscriminate killing of leopards for the trade in skins that later prompted the authorities in most of the Central African territories to place the leopard on the protected list. With the extermination of so many of the great cats the balance of nature was soon upset and baboons, their favourite prey, increased to such alarming proportions that they became a positive menace to the native population. Plantations were systematically raided and denuded by the apes, and on several occasions native women and children were savagely attacked when they tried to drive the raiders from their fields.

It is many years since I last had one of the spotted cats running around the house; this is not due to a lack of interest in them, but to the difficulty in finding adequate meat supplies to keep them well fed.

CHAPTER XVII

SMALL BUT DANGEROUS

W HEN REFERENCE IS made to the buffalo in stories of adventure, the reader's mind generally turns to the Cape buffalo (*Cynerus Caffer*). That perhaps is as it should be, for the Cape buffalo, the bad boy of the African forest, has provided plenty of material for hunters to write about, and for anyone who is in search of first-rate adventure he is always a suitable adversary to fall back upon.

But there is a prototype of the Cape species of which one seldom hears, and that is the little red buffalo of the Congo forest. Much smaller than the Cape buffalo, and with a completely different horn formation, he is in fact quite as dangerous as his larger brother; in those parts of the Congo where he is frequently hunted he has earned for himself the reputation of being every bit as vicious and aggressive as the rhino, who is inclined to charge on scent.

This peculiarity of the rhino does not really stamp him as a very dangerous animal, for his charge as a rule is the result of muddled reasoning. By no means over-burdened with brains, and afflicted with defective eye-sight which prevents him from seeing much farther than ten yards, he will charge anything that seems foreign to his smell. If he misses his charge and gets above the wind of his imagined enemy, he is quite satisfied that the danger has been removed, and after a little futile sniffing of the air he will go on his way, believing that all is well.

No buffalo, black or red, is ever guilty of such shoddy workmanship. For some reason which is not very clear, the Congo red buffalo is nothing like so prolific a breeder as the Cape buffalo, and whereas the latter was almost entirely wiped out in Central, East and South

Africa during the great rinderpest epidemic of 1897, there is nothing on record to prove that the red buffalo was affected very seriously by the disease. Up to the time of the great rinderpest epidemic the Cape buffalo was essentially an animal of the open plains, but after the epidemic they took to the forest regions, emerging into the open only when they came to water late in the afternoons or in the hours just before daybreak. The red buffalo, by all accounts, has *always* favoured the dense forest and is only rarely to be seen on the open plains.

It is possibly due to the difficult country he frequents, his evil temper and his tendency to charge without direct provocation, that the natives in the Congo have always shown a disinclination to hunt him, and no native will accompany a European on his trail unless he feels reasonably certain of the white man's ability to deal effectively with this aggressive little fellow.

It was after some years of hunting in the Congo that I once organised a small safari in the Lualaba district to go in search of the red buffalo. Apart from the excitement such an adventure offered, I was anxious to obtain a good pair of horns for a collection I was making for an American museum at the time. I had considerable trouble in collecting the right type of trackers and spotters, for apart from their reluctance to have anything to do with the hunting of the " red devil " on account of his aggressiveness, many of the native tribes in those parts refuse to hunt him on superstitious grounds—a superstition that extends not only to the hunting of this animal, but also to the eating of his meat.

Once on the trail, I soon discovered that the red buffalo had several distinctive characteristics that made him a much more difficult animal to hunt than the Cape buffalo. These were his tendency to roam over large areas, and a lack of inclination to settle down for long in one spot. The well-worn trails we came across all indicated that he favoured the densest parts of the forest, and unlike the black buffalo, herds rarely exceeded ten or twelve animals. On a couple of occasions we came across comparatively fresh tracks late in the morning, but on both occasions the trail had to be abandoned in the afternoons without seeing a trace of the quarry. Then, early one morning, we got on to fresh tracks. There had been a heavy drizzle during the night and the soft ground made trailing quite easy for the trackers. Luck also favoured us, in that we followed the trail " up-wind ", and success depended almost entirely on the ability of the spotters to locate the herd before they became aware of our presence.

We stuck to the trail for more than an hour in extremely dense forest, and then suddenly there were signs of more open country ahead of us. It was as we reached the edge of an open clearing in the dense bush that a herd was spotted grazing in a patch of green grass. The range was roughly 200 yards, and I would have preferred to reduce the distance before taking a shot, but I decided it would be better to take the chance over the longer distance than taking a risk of being seen if I came into the open.

After looking over the herd carefully, I selected the largest bull, and lining him up carefully in my sights, I squeezed the trigger of the heavy ·404 calibre rifle I was using. The shot was apparently well placed on the shoulder, for the bull went down in a heap where he stood. The herd made off at a fast pace, and another big bull which I had hoped to bag disappeared in the close bush before I could train my sights on him properly.

No sooner had the bull gone down when one of my Swahili natives rushed out, knife in hand, so as to be in time to cut the throat of the animal before it was properly dead. This would render the meat safe to eat in accordance with their religion. Quite satisfied that the bull was dead, I walked slowly on the trail of the native, not taking any particular notice of him or the buffalo. Suddenly my attention was drawn to loud shouting ahead of me, and I saw the native make a wild swerve and head for the nearest tree on his right. Some fifty yards behind him was the bull in hot pursuit.

For a moment I was not unduly disturbed, as the native was quite close to the tree and normally should have got out of reach before the bull caught up with him, for the average native has nothing to learn from the apes in climbing trees when there is trouble brewing with a buffalo. I tried a second shot, which missed the target completely and failed to put the buffalo off its course. By now the native had reached the tree and some twenty yards still separated the two. Already he had started his climb as the bull approached him, bellowing loudly. Compared with what I had seen previously in similar circumstances, this native was crawling up the tree at a pace of a mile a month. The relative positions of the two now made it unsafe for me to try another shot, for fear of endangering the man's life, should I miss the target.

When the buffalo reached the tree, the native was still hanging on grimly for life, but he was barely out of reach of the bull's horns and kept screaming for help at the top of his voice. The bull, fortunately, was so intent upon settling his score with the native that he did not notice my approach, and a few seconds later I brought proceedings to an end with a heavy slug in his neck.

What had happened on this occasion was that the trunk of the tree was too large to negotiate easily, and in addition it was studded with heavy curved thorns by which the native's trousers were hooked and held in a vice-like grip, and this made it impossible for him to move.

My first bullet had struck the shoulder too high, and the shock of the impact had momentarily paralysed the bull. But after he had recovered from the shock he appeared none the worse for wear. After it was all over the unfortunate victim was subjected to the usual bantering by the other members of the safari, but I should have hated to have occupied his unenviable position in the tree for those few minutes before the bull was finally accounted for—more so in view of the fact that he was fast losing his grip on the trunk, and hit the ground only a second or two after the bull was shot.

During the rest of the safari I collected three more good specimens, but none of them provided any worthwhile excitement. In later years I shot a good many more of the little "red devils", but always without any untoward incident, and if it were not for the fact that several experienced European hunters have fared so badly when hunting them, I should not subscribe to the belief that the little " red devil " is such a dangerous animal to hunt.

Another animal with a great reputation for cunning and ferocity, but who failed to run true to form on the only occasion I hunted him, is the black panther of Abyssinia. As in the case of the black and red buffalo and the black and green mamba, it is claimed that the black panther is, in fact, a true leopard and that the colouring is only a variation of type. If these creatures of different appearance are all true representatives of one species, it would appear that they lose a good many of their inherent traits in the process of " variation ". Although they may be quite as dangerous as the more commonly known types, they somehow fail to fill the headlines where really dangerous animals are concerned. When buffalo are discussed as being very dangerous animals, it is generally the black type that comes to mind and not the red. When the deadly mamba is discussed, it is generally the black species that fills the role of the great killer, and not the green; and whereas it is probably quite true that they are identically the same but for the colouring, it is also true that quite seventy-five per cent of the victims of a green mamba are generally saved, the black mamba kills ninety-five times in a hundred at least; and as for aggressiveness, there is no comparison.

In the matter of choice as to which of the two leopards —spotted or black—is the more dangerous, my one hunt of the latter obviously does not qualify me to pass judgement, but I do know that every species of animal follows instinctive traits—especially in times of danger—and can be relied upon to show their true colours when wounded or aggravated. It is in this respect that I found the black panther a far more docile and less impulsive creature than his spotted brother.

I made my trip to Abyssinia in order to collect firsthand material for a book on that country, and whilst there I met my old friend Major Darley, whose book *Slaves and Ivory* created a great sensation when it was first published. At that time he was acting as Frontier Agent on the Abyssinian–Sudanese border. The Major was a keen hunter, and was only too anxious to accompany me in search of a good specimen of black panther. He belonged to the old school of sportsman-hunter who saw no harm in setting bait and waiting for an outlaw animal at night, but in hunting for a trophy, he insisted that it had to be done the right way, which, in the case of leopards, was also the hard way, and that was to track the quarry down in the day-time.

During that week we went out daily in search of a panther, and we must have walked well over 100 miles without seeing a sign of one. Then, late one afternoon, after I had given up all hope of ever finding one, our luck turned and we spotted one trotting slowly across a little clearing. He was apparently following the trail of some small animal and was quite unaware of our presence. For this outing I had brought along a shotgun and also a ·275 Magnum Express rifle. The distance was too great for a shotgun, and I soon had the panther lined up in the sights of the Express.

As I fired the shot a puff of dust could be seen rising on the other side of the panther, who made a tremendous leap and disappeared in the close bush before I could fire another shot. None of us had heard the bullet strike, and there was nothing in the panther's leap that suggested he had been hit. We were all certain that I had missed the target, and immediately started following in the direction it had taken to make sure there was no blood on the trail.   There was no sign anywhere and it was quite impossible to find any tracks in the tangled undergrowth.

For some distance we walked haphazardly, in the forlorn hope that it might show up again.   We had just come to a particularly dense cluster of bush when my attention was drawn to the sound of spitting and snarling a few yards ahead of me.   As I looked in the direction of the sound I spotted the panther a little more than ten yards away.   Although he was in a crouching attitude, he had up to that point made no attempt to attack, and before he could do so I placed a bullet between his eyes and he rolled over dead.

On examining the carcass we found that the first bullet had gone clean through the stomach without striking bone, and although painful, it was by no means a crippling wound, and it could not have prevented him from attacking me once I had approached him so closely. A member of the spotted type, I feel certain, would never have allowed me to come anywhere near him without attacking, and it is doubtful if he would have made any attempt to escape after he was hit in the first place. There is no animal in the bush that I know of that resents injury as actively as do the spotted cats.

However, this was but one experience, and there may be many hunters with a very different story to tell.   On one point, however, we are all agreed, and that is that the black panther does not take second place to his spotted brother in the matter of beauty.   Mine was a superb specimen, and the trophy amply repaid me for all the trouble I had in collecting it.   One of my greatest desires for years after this adventure was to collect a small cub to train as a pet, and although I made elaborate arrangements before my departure, my luck in this respect did not hold.

CHAPTER XVIII

BANGI PAYS A DEBT

M Y HUNTING AND prospecting activities during the years have on two occasions brought me in close personal touch with the most revolting of all the denizens of the forest—the cannibal. One occasion was far up in the Ubangi country, where I saw these savages in their native haunts and narrowly escaped their attentions; the other was on the Lualaba River in the Belgian Congo when I went in search of a prospector who was several days overdue at headquarters, and it was feared that he had fallen victim to a truculent native chief named Katapemba.

Katapemba was an aggressive native who had a distinct dislike of Europeans, and although he himself may not have practised cannibalism actively, he certainly took no steps to suppress the evil habit in the district over which he ruled. Before going on this trip I had asked for, and was supplied with, a bodyguard of four Matabele natives who had served in the police force in Southern Rhodesia, and who were armed with service model rifles. With such potent assistance I was not unduly alarmed when, on camping close to Katapemba's kraal, I received a message from him telling me that my presence was unwelcome and that if I did not vacate the vicinity forthwith he would take the necessary steps to make sure that I conformed with his wishes.

When I called on Katapemba later in the day, accompanied by my armed bodyguard, his attitude changed very perceptibly and he explained that the threat earlier in the day was merely a harmless joke. Before returning to my camp I was presented with a goat—the customary peace offering of the tribe. I was not greatly impressed with Katapemba's peaceful gesture and explained to him the object of my visit to his district, emphasising the fact that I would be on my way early the next morning.

He told me that Hooke, the missing prospector, had passed that way some three weeks earlier and to the best of his knowledge he was well and prospecting in the Lufupa area, some hundred miles to the north. It was on my way to Lufupa two days later that I once again came across the gruesome evidence of active cannibalism, when I arrived at a small village deep in the forest early one morning. The village was deserted by all but a few aged women who spoke a dialect which none of us understood. Before leaving the village I instructed the Matabeles to examine every hut carefully and look for any evidence that could have any connection with the missing prospector.

A few minutes later one of the Matabeles came to me and asked me to follow him to a hut at the far end of the village. On arriving there I saw a number of ropes stretched between posts planted firmly in the ground. Tied to these ropes were several pieces of human flesh, the black skin in each case testifying to the fact the victim was a native who had been killed quite recently. Whilst looking at this gruesome sight my attention was drawn to the sounds of groaning and moaning in a nearby hut, the door of which was securely fastened on the outside.

With the help of the Matabeles the door was quickly broken down. The interior of the hut was in complete darkness. Flashing my torch-light to the corner from where the groans came, I looked into the terrified eyes of a native child of perhaps eight or nine years of age. His arms and legs were securely bound and tied to a post inside the hut. He obviously was the intended victim of the next cannibal feast and, as I discovered later, the son of the man whose flesh hung suspended over the ropes outside.

I handed the torch to one of my native guards whilst I proceeded to unsheath my hunting-knife and approached the youth. Seeing a white man in normal circumstances would have been a terrifying experience for a native child in those parts, for white men rarely if ever frequented that part of the country, and this child, in all probability, had never seen a white man before. Seeing this white ogre, knife in hand, approaching him in his desperate plight, must have petrified him with fear, for with his eyes wide open and staring at me with horror, he let out screams of terror that have lived with me over the many years that have passed since.

Cutting loose the bonds that held him was quite a simple matter, but the moment he realised that he was free, the poor little wretch crawled towards me and, grabbing me around the legs, he set up a pathetic wail, pleading desperately for mercy. His wide-open eyes and Arab-like features were filled with terror, but seeing me return the knife to its sheath helped to pacify him, and the wailing ceased. His language was foreign to us all, for he spoke one of the native dialects of that part of the Congo. Although we could not understand a word of what he said, he made us understand by signals that he was hungry and thirsty. His needs were immediately attended to, and I lost no further time in getting the safari on the way.

Once well beyond the confines of the village, my porters came to a sudden stop and demanded a discussion on this latest development. The spokesman of the group stated that they were not prepared to continue the journey with the child in our midst. The country, he declared, was inhabited not only by cannibals, but also by Leopard Men, who they feared even more than they did the cannibals, and whereas they were satisfied that we were well enough equipped to protect ourselves during the day, they were afraid of the night. They felt certain that we should be subjected to an attack during the hours of darkness. The only way to avert such trouble, they claimed, was to leave the boy to his fate, and they insisted that this be done before we continued our journey.

The Matabeles accompanying me were trained men on whom I could rely and they were well supplied with ammunition. On being assured that they were prepared to see the business through, I told the spokesman who had delivered the ultimatum that I was determined to take the boy with me. I was also quite content to leave all those who refused to follow us to the tender mercies of the cannibals and Leopard Men. Without firearms for protection the outlook for them would be grim. My form of reasoning had the desired results, and we made camp that night a good ten miles from the horror village.

Shortly before dark I arranged to have sentries posted at vantage points in the dark and gave instructions that there was to be no shooting without my permission except in case of an attack. It was close to midnight when the first dark, shadowy form could be seen in the glare of the camp-fire.

" He is carrying a bow and arrows," shouted one of the sentries.

I immediately fired a shot in the direction of the vanishing form, but in the dim light I missed the target. An hour later the performance was repeated, with similar results. For the rest of the night there were several more visits, but I thought it advisable not to try to hit the intruders, but merely let them know that we were on the alert by firing in their direction. By daybreak we had suffered nothing more serious than a poisoned arrow which had fallen harmlessly near the camp-fire.

During the next five days we made good progress without further molestation until we came near another village, the chief of which belonged to the Mabunda tribe. It was in this vicinity that I expected to find Hooke. Shortly after we had settled in camp I sent a messenger to the chief, advising him of our arrival and asking him to call on me. This chief, whose name I have now forgotten, was an even more truculent type of native than Katapemba, and he promptly ordered a few of his men to chase the messenger from his village. I decided I would call on the chief a little later in company with my armed guard, but before I could start on my way to the village, the news leaked through that Hooke was actually laid up in a hut there.

On receiving this news I immediately called out the Matabeles and proceeded to the village. The appearance of so much armed force at the door of his hut had a soothing influence on the chief's temper, and he offered the information that Hooke was being taken care of in a nearby hut. He had been carried to the village several days earlier, suffering from a severe dose of malaria fever. A few moments later I was taken to the hut, where I found Hooke lying on a rough camp-bed. He had, in fact, suffered a bad attack of fever and had been taken care of by the chief, but during the time he had spent in the village the chief had told him on several occasions that they would fatten him up so that he would provide a good feast in the near future. On questioning the chief about this he laughingly admitted that it was true, but, as in the case of Katapemba, it was all done in a joke. I did not think it advisable to stay in the vicinity too long, and two days later we were on our journey back home.

By this time Bangi had fully recovered from his alarming experience in the cannibal village, and, like all natives in those parts, he was rapidly picking up words in the Swahili language. It was, however, quite a month before we could get a connected account from him as to the events that preceded his landing in the village.

His story followed a familiar pattern. A group of cannibals had raided deep into his country, and whilst he and his father were walking on a footpath to visit a nearby village they were suddenly attacked by these savages. Both were securely tied together and taken to the village where we found him. Shortly after their arrival there, he had seen his father killed by spears and

he was taken to the hut from which we had rescued him.
He was quite aware of the fact that they had fallen
victims to cannibals, and the time he had spent in the
hut had been a nightmare experience for him, for he
lived in dread all the time that he would be taken out at
any moment and killed in the same manner as his father.

Even with his limited vocabulary, he made me understand that he owed me a debt of gratitude which he
would never forget.   As time went on he became more
fluent in Swahili, and he often dwelt on that day when I
had rescued him from the cannibals.   He frequently
assured me that he would never leave me.   As the years
went by he often repeated this assurance, and on several
occasions he emphasised his loyalty by telling me that if
ever I needed him in a time of danger I would always
find him at hand.

During the next fifteen years I hunted buffaloes
assiduously, and Bangi accompanied me on most of these
outings.   He had by now grown into a sturdy young
man and learnt a great deal of the technique of buffalo-
hunting.   He always carried a rifle when he accompanied me, but he was never a success as a shot or as a
tracker.   But as a " spotter " he soon outstripped most
of the others, and for this reason he became one of the
most reliable members of my hunting staff.   He was a
cheerful soul and devoted his entire life to me and my
welfare.

The memories of those days in the cannibal hut, however, never faded entirely from his mind, for whenever
he became involved in a dispute with other members of
the staff he would have his say and conclude the argument by telling the other party to the dispute that he was
" only a cannibal ", an insult which often aggravated
matters.

Whilst on the buffalo trail there were many incidents
and narrow escapes.   These incidents generally brought
serious remonstrances from Bangi for what he considered
was carelessness and recklessness on my part.   Then

there came the day when I had the narrowest escape of all and I averted disaster by the proverbial skin of my teeth. As usual, the trackers and porters had made for the tree-tops as soon as the trouble started. Bangi, as a spotter, was some distance from the scene of the trouble, but had watched proceedings with a critical eye.

That night as I sat outside my tent door he came up to me and seated himself beside me. " Bwana," he began, " since that day when you saved me from the cannibals I have never disobeyed you, and that is why I walk with the spotters every day. But from now onwards I do not wish to walk with them any more. Today I saw what happened: those cannibals all rushed up into the trees when you were in danger. You were lucky that the big bull fell down dead before he could turn on you after you got out of his way. If he had turned back on his tracks he would surely have killed you, and none of those cowards would have been near enough to fire a shot to help you. From tomorrow onwards I wish to carry a gun and walk close to you. If trouble comes I will not run for the trees. All the men here say that it is only a matter of time before you will be killed because you take too many risks. I know they are right, for the god of the forest has often told me that I will be the one to save you from one of those black devils."

If the " god of the forest " had decreed that Bangi was destined to save me from a charging buffalo he never-theless failed to provide him with the opportunity. For a few more years we hunted regularly; Bangi was always close to me with his rifle in hand, and on the few occasions when charges developed he stood his ground, but I was always lucky to keep out of trouble without his help. But time was beginning to take its toll. My eyes and nerves began to suffer from the strain of dangerous hunting. There came the day when, after another nerve-wrecking experience, I decided to " call it a day " where buffalo-hunting was concerned. Bangi was happy when I told him of my decision, but still kept on brooding over his bad luck in not having had an opportunity of saving me from serious trouble with a buffalo.

We were then in Tanganyika Territory, where I had gone to join the famous gold rush on the Lupa, and here I hunted only for the pot whilst playing my luck at alluvial gold. Of all my old hunting crew only Black and Bangi remained. Black was employed in the field with a gang of labourers, whilst Bangi attended to my creature comforts in a lonely hut on the field. The country was fever-ridden, and before long I was in the throes of a severe dose of intermittent malaria. Each afternoon my temperature would rise alarmingly, and this brought on spells of delirium.

I had just come out of one of these spells one afternoon with Bangi sitting beside my bed when there was a sudden " flop " on the floor in the centre of the hut. On looking in the direction of the disturbance I was horrified to see a black mamba with fully one third of its body raised from the ground. It had adopted a most menacing attitude with head swaying to and fro and the beady eyes staring in our direction.

In a flash Bangi, with a stick in hand, rushed at the snake. As he lashed out at the snake and missed I saw the deadly reptile fasten its fangs in his arm. Another vicious blow from Bangi and the snake lay wriggling on the floor with a broken back.

" He's finished now, Bwana; he can do no more harm," Bangi said as he showed me the blood oozing from the fang-wounds.

I attended to him as quickly as I could in my weak state; cauterized the wound, tied a ligature above his elbow and injected a powerful dose of serum. " Why did you go near the snake, Bangi? Why did you not leave him alone? He would have calmed down and left us alone if you did not disturb him," I said.

" No, Bwana," he replied; " did you not see that he was ready to attack? When a mamba swings his head like this one did and sticks out his tongue, nothing will stop him from biting. It was lucky that I was here to stop him, otherwise he would surely have killed you," he replied.

"But you, Bangi, what about you?"

"Oh, that is nothing, Bwana; the medicine you have injected will help me and I will be all right."

But Bangi was not all right. An hour later the deadly symptoms began to appear. I knew just what that meant: there was nothing more I could do to save him. A few minutes later I was back in the throes of yet another spell of delirium. When I awoke from it, I do not know how long after, I called frantically, "Bangi! Bangi!!" But there was no reply, and I knew that Bangi would never answer my call again. So the "god of the forest" was right, but it was not from the horns of an enraged buffalo that he had saved me, but from the fangs of a deadly reptile. Bangi had paid his debt. Farewell, brave, loyal little Bangi. "Greater love hath no man . . ."

CHAPTER XIX

CHE SARÀ, SARÀ

In the old Park days, which I have written about elsewhere, my companions, for the want of something better to do, passed most of their leisure hours reading books on philosophy, theology, etc. It was inevitable that I, too, should follow the fashion and dig deep into the problems of life and death. After I had read most of the famous rationalists, from Voltaire downwards, I delved deep into the works of writers on the other side of the fence. After I had finished these I tossed all the books overboard, so to speak, in complete bewilderment. Both sides understood these questions differently, but both sides understood them best.

For myself, I went to a bookseller and bought a copy of *The Rubaiyat of Omar Khayyam*, a book which I have carried with me all these years. Omar does not give one the impression that he believed in anything very definite, except to keep going whilst the going is good. His philosophy, I suppose, is as good as most others, and I have found very little in it to quarrel about, but as time went on I found it convenient to add a little philosophy of my own—" Fatalism "—which perhaps is not so much a philosophy as a state of mind.

If anyone were to ask me to explain how Fatalism operates I would not know how to begin, but that does not alter the fact that I believe implicitly in the maxim *Che sarà, sarà*—" What will be, will be." My old friend Mickey Norton, who never missed an opportunity to score against me, was never greatly impressed with this prognostication, and had a much simpler explanation to offer when I discussed with him my many narrow escapes in the bush.

Mickey was convinced that Old Man Satan was not

anxious to accommodate me, for fear I might lead his other guests astray. The old saying about true words being spoken in jest may be right, and perhaps he had something there. Why this homily on philosophy in a book that deals with adventures in the bush? It is because, sitting meditating a few nights ago, it occurred to me that, for some reason or other, fate has so decreed it that I am not booked for a violent end in the bush. Heaven alone knows, by all the rules of the game, I should have had my deserts on a good many occasions.

There was that occasion when a herd of running buffalo presented an easy target and I emptied a magazine of five rounds on them and saw two animals go down. I had no particular reason to believe that I had scored more than two hits; the cloud of dust and the confused manner in which the animals ran made accurate observation quite impossible. They were making for an open plain at the side of which, some 300 yards ahead of me, stood an enormous tree.

After checking up on the two kills, I decided I would go up to the tree and climb on to its highest branches, from where I could check up with a pair of powerful binoculars and make sure there was no animal trailing behind, as they usually do when severely wounded. I had just reached the tree, and stood looking up to see which would be the easiest way to climb on to the first protruding limb, when there was a loud, long-drawn-out grunt in the thick grass on the other side of the tree— not more than five yards from me. What I had heard was the last dying grunt of a monster bull who had shipped a heavy ·425-calibre bullet through both lungs, ran 300 yards, and lived until I had reached the tree before giving up the ghost. If I had spent less time examining the two dead animals there would have been a very different story.

Then there was the day when I foolishly believed a wounded bull had stuck to the herd and gone to the far end of a patch of thick grass. I was walking slowly on the tracks of the herd, following a fresh blood-trail on the grass ahead of me. Suddenly an uncanny feeling came over me that all was not well, and as I looked sideways it was to stare into the scowling face of the bull, barely an arm's length from me. Was it fate, or did that bull think that it was not worth while wasting his time on me? Before I could recover from my shock he snorted viciously, swerved round on his hind legs and made off into the dense grass. For some seconds I stood there rooted to the ground, paralysed with shock; then I raised my helmet and banged myself hard on the head three times to make quite sure that it was not a nightmare from which I had just awakened.

How can I explain that afternoon when I had wounded a topi in the open plain and followed the blood-trail for fully two miles before it entered thick grass? So dense was the grass that visibility was reduced to a bare three yards ahead. For fully 200 yards I had struggled through this dense foliage when I pushed down yet another cluster—to stare into the eyes of a huge male lion two yards from me. He was busy helping himself to my topi. When that lion snarled viciously and rushed off in a great hurry, I stood watching the grass being trampled down for what I thought was an hour. At the end of that time I thought it would be as well for me to resume the business of breathing!

As we are on the subject of lions, there was that other incident which I have described in full detail elsewhere. I had sent a heavy ·425 slug through what I believed was the chest of the brute and knocked him flat. A few minutes later he was back on all fours and entered thick scrub. I was wise enough not to follow him into this death-trap and decided to throw stones in his direction from a safe distance and await further developments. It was whilst I was busy trying to dig out a suitable stone that I was brought face to face with reality as the snarling beast came for me with open jaws. There was no time to shoot, and I sprinted off at right-angles to the charge.

It was as the lion swerved from his straight course to follow me that he collapsed and rolled over dead. I was not aware at the time what had happened, and kept running at top speed until I fell in a heap seventy-five yards farther on. For fully a year I lived almost nightly through this adventure in nightmare dreams.

Perhaps it was fate that intervened that day on Lake Rukwa when I followed a school of hippos in a native canoe in order to secure a good specimen for an American museum. For over an hour their heads kept bobbing up and down in different places. The native boatman was having a terrific struggle steering and turning the boat in the wake of the wily hippos. Now a fine big bull had surfaced, and I was sitting on the edge of the boat trying to get in a brain-shot when the boat suddenly swerved. I could not fire my shot from the deep water where I had landed, but swam frantically to regain the boat. One leg was already in the boat, and as I lifted the other over the side, the jaws of a monster-size crocodile snapped to as he grazed the heel of my shoe. The only redeeming feature of this incident was that from the position I occupied I was saved the unpleasant sight of looking into those wide-open jaws as the brute snapped at me. That would have been too reminiscent of the day when I looked down the throat of a huge puff-adder as his jaws snapped to. The width of tissue paper separated those deadly fangs from my knee. I had offended him by tramping on his tail. Later that day I got my hippo, but when I fired that shot I was sitting down flat, right in the centre of the canoe.

Another terrifying incident occurred when Black, my old gun-bearer, and I followed the trail of a wounded elephant. We were in dense forest, and trailing had become a sticky business—so much so that Black's nerves began to get edgy and he signalled to me that he was not prepared to go deeper into the close bush. I decided to follow the trail a little farther before abandoning the pursuit. I had just come to a large tree when the bull must have seen or scented me. He immediately went through all the preliminaries of a charge, stretched his ears wide, lifted his trunk high, set up a loud squeal, and then came in my direction.

He was still a good forty yards from me, but " local " conditions were not satisfactory. The numerous obstructions in the line of fire would have made shooting a tricky and risky business. The only other thing to do was to " freeze hard " against the trunk of the tree. Elephants have very poor eyesight, and, unlike the buffalo, they generally charge with their heads well raised, and in this manner they will invariably rush past a stationary object if the wind is not in their favour. I promptly went into a " freeze ", and when that bull rushed past me I could easily have slapped his hind quarters.

Black also was a pastmaster at " freezing ", and as I looked at the bull running towards him I saw that he was absolutely still. Then suddenly he made a wild leap away from the tree; it was then that the bull lifted him in his trunk and tossed him high. As soon as the bull turned round to complete his work of destruction I went into action with a heavy ·475 elephant gun. The first shot, between the eyes—of no great value where elephants are concerned—brought the bull to a momentary stop and gave me time to place another bullet which entered the brain and brought him down as Black crawled away on all fours. He was badly bruised all over his body, but luckily no bones were broken.

" You were quite safe where you stood against the tree, Black; whatever possessed you to jump right into the way of a charging elephant? " I queried.

" You see, Bwana," he replied, " I did not have time to examine that tree properly before I stood against it, and I did not notice a nest of hornets above my head. Eh, Bwana, when a swarm of those devils dig into your skin you don't have time to think about charging elephants."

It is true, there is no special reason to invoke fate in

this case, for I was never in any really great danger, but I might have been had our positions been reversed that day, for Black was never a great shot and I should have hated to depend on him shooting when there is dirty work at the cross-roads with an infuriated elephant bull at work!

Another time when an elephant had me at his mercy and must have decided that it would not be " cricket " to take advantage of my helpless position was when I was after buffalo. I had followed a native footpath which led down a thirty-feet-steep bank of the Sira River in Tanganyika. The brush was so dense beside and above the path, which was less than a foot wide, that visibility was reduced to zero. I had slung my rifle over my shoulder and crawled down the bank on all fours. Suddenly my attention was drawn to a movement right in front of me. Perhaps I should not have been so alarmed, for it was only a big bull elephant, followed by madam elephant, who was climbing up the steep bank on the same narrow footpath. I was shocked into immobility, and for a few seconds I sat looking into the bull's eyes. I was still thinking which would be the best prayer to resort to when he turned round and walked down the path slowly behind madam as though it was the most normal thing in all the world.

It was much later that afternoon that I again encountered this magnanimous couple in very different circumstances, for the pair were trapped in a ring of fire set by native hunters. I was able to repay their generous gesture of the morning by stopping the native hunters who were already closing in with their muzzle-loaders. After a long palaver accompanied by threats and promises to make amends for the loss of meat, I persuaded them to hold their fire. But I could not do anything to help the elephants to escape from their unenviable position. To have approached them in order to extinguish the fire would have been the height of folly. But, as it turned out, they did not really need my help.

I stood watching them from a safe distance as they kept wheeling round in a panic of fear.   At last, as the flames were almost licking their sides, I saw them draw water from their stomachs with their trunks and extinguish the flames.   A few moments later they broke out of the ring of fire and went on their way, and left me to redeem my promise to make amends.   Thinking it over, I feel that it might not have been so healthy for me had I met that couple on the narrow footpath *after* the fire incident!

There have been so many other incidents in the hunting field which I have related elsewhere that this last one, which had nothing to do with hunting, will not be out of place.   It was after a long and tedious march during the East African campaign that my friend Bryan and I were detailed to form part of a sentry group in an outlying position that night.   The long march earlier in the day had so fatigued my friend that he asked me to change places with him and take his shift from 8 p.m. till 10 p.m.   At ten o'clock Bryan turned out to relieve me; half an hour later a shot rang out in the dark.   We all rushed out to man our positions, and were horrified to find Bryan lying dead at his post.   He had shipped an 11-mm. bullet through both lungs.   That would have been my fate but for the last-minute change in mounting guard for the night.

When I think of all the incidents I have related here and elsewhere, I cannot help but believe that fate has excluded my name from the list of those who are due to come to a violent end.   I am writing this on the island of Majorca, where we have no elephants, buffalo, lions or other dangerous animals, and to that extent my chances have improved, and I feel reasonably safe.   But I go up-town every morning for my daily paper, and I have heard of cases where people have slipped on a banana skin and died from concussion of the brain. *Che sarà, sarà.*